GETTING

EXTRA-ORDINARY RESULTS FROM ORDINARY PEOPLE

(or Be a Purple Banana)

BY JEZ ROSE

Be a Purple Banana
Getting Extraordinary Results from Ordinary People
By Jez Rose

Jez Rose has asserted his right in accordance
with the Copyright, Designs and Patents Act 1988
to be identified as the author of this work.

First published in Great Britain in 2015
by Dr. Zeus Publishing

Printed in Great Britain

Set in Electra LT Regular

Dr. Zeus Publishing
c/o 7 Merlin Centre
Aylesbury
Buckinghamshire
HP19 8DP

ISBN: 978-0-9930136-2-1

Cover design and production: Claire Speight
Photography: Alex Healy
Editor: Wendy Mansfield

For Gwendoline Pearl Cunliffe - Grandma.
Thank you for the happiness and for being such
a perfect catalyst for extraordinary.

CONTENTS

INTRODUCTION

"I wish I could show you,
when you are lonely or in
darkness, the astonishing
light of your own being."

Hafiz, Persian poet.

Normal is Taken

 I remember where I was; it was a large stately home just outside of Birmingham. The sort you'd see on television and pass comment on: deep oak panelled walls; flagstone floors; large fireplaces that were so big you could fit a table into and use as a novelty dining area; suits of armour nonchalantly displayed in corners - you know the sort. I had just spoken to a group of about six hundred sales people about how to deliver extraordinary levels of customer service and the psychological affects it has on customers. I remember that clearly. I don't remember, however, who it was, but they pointed at my moustache, smiled and said: "I love that!" I thanked them and they replied: "I think that's brilliant! Do many people stare at you?" A little taken aback at the notion of being positioned as something of a freak show by a complete stranger, I confirmed that it occasionally got an odd look from a narrow-minded individual; those people who lead an alarmingly sheltered life if a curly moustache is the most remarkable or offensive thing they've ever seen. But otherwise, it draws more smiles and approving looks than the former. The person, whoever it was, then went on to say: "Brilliant! And why not, hey? Normal is taken!"

It was at that moment that time quite literally stood still for me. I stood next to a window the size of the entrance of an aircraft hangar with its lush, heavy drapes as people walked on by, while I simply stared. Normal is taken. Indeed it is. My mind began racing with questions to answer. Why would anyone want to be ordinary? Do people consciously know that they are ordinary? What is ordinary? What is extraordinary? Why wouldn't you be extraordinary if you had the choice? How do you become extraordinary? And then, for the next four years, often consciously and nearly always subconsciously I started analysing everyday interactions between people; people's responses to situations; listening to and reviewing how they presented themselves, spoke about themselves and the choices and decisions they made and their responses to the consequences of those choices. My professional library contains over three thousand books, many of them devoted to body language, the human brain, behaviour and psychology.

Many of them were purchased within the past four years as my research into all of those questions about ordinary and extraordinary began to border on the obsessive. You know you're obsessed by something when people ask your fiancée about you and your obsession instead of asking you because they are scared to. As a behaviourist, however, this innate interest and desire to observe and quantify behaviour in an attempt to further understand it is unstoppable and is as much a part of me as my eyes.

During my attempts to understand what extraordinary was, it quickly became obvious, to me at least, that if "normal was taken," there were huge commercial reasons that supported being extraordinary in business and that for very different reason, being extraordinary as a provider of education, if you are a teacher or lecturer, for example, had potentially life changing implications. The more I thought about the notion of not being like everyone else, of striving to be extraordinary in what you do, I realised that there were important lessons for us all to consider. But I didn't set out to write this book. I was bullied into it in a way. I actually only wanted to write one book, but my first book, now long out of print, was a collaborative effort and I later found out that my co-author's content was taken from a licence-free book. So I wrote a book on my own, however, *Have a Crap Day* was an unexpected success that resulted in lots more people communicating and interacting with me. And as a result of those many wonderful conversations with people all over the world, I learned that what was perfectly normal to some; the ways in which some people contextualise things; their viewpoints; outlooks on life and ways of managing certain situations and behaviours, were actually quite extra-ordinary to others. And I mean extraordinary in the literal sense, not the self-righteous sense nonchalantly muttered by people wearing loafers with a jumper casually slung around their shoulders as they run their hand through their overly wavy hair. So, I find myself here writing another book. I felt I ought to qualify the history of how this book came about, in case you mistook me for a bearded version of Jilly Cooper, churning out books quicker than you can say 'riding crop'.

I wanted this book to answer three fundamental questions I had about this notion of being extraordinary; they are:

1. Why be extraordinary?
2. What is the difference between ordinary
   and extraordinary?
3. How does one become extraordinary?

It's a wonderful fact of life that every single day, ordinary people do extraordinary things: carrying out extraordinary acts and creating extraordinary results. Although, it's perhaps a more accurate statement that in reality, some ordinary people sometimes can do extraordinary things. Which isn't as inspiring a statement, however, I genuinely believe that each of us has the ability to be extraordinary and create extraordinary things. You may well be reading this and thinking: "well, you've clearly never met my sister," or "if you'd met Uncle Barry you wouldn't be saying that." However, as I'll hopefully show you, even those people you've given up all hope for, are capable of performing at an extraordinary level.

Let me get one thing clear though, this is not a vacuous, fanciful statement used simply to make you feel good about yourself. One thing I don't want this book to be is insincere without any soul. For the past ten years I've been presenting to organisations worldwide and asking members of those audiences, ranging from fifty to three thousand people at a time, from all sorts of backgrounds and industries, ranging from pharmaceutical, manufacturing, hospitality, education and finance: "how many of you are specialists in your field?" The first few times I asked, hardly anyone put their hand up - less than one percent of the audience. I wouldn't say I was shocked, however, I was a little surprised. Now, granted, lots of people don't willingly interact with speakers or in presentations, however, even when pushed, the vast majority sat there in silence, staring blankly back at me. So I started to ask that same question in every presentation, workshop and seminar I gave. I wanted to see what sort of variations there were in the responses I received. The response didn't change when asked to teachers, lawyers, doctors, sales representatives, research assistants and management teams; it was the same hesitance and is so to this day when I ask that very same question. While you may not be the country's leading surgeon, or the head of department, or revered by your peers for specialised research and you may be all too aware of people much more qualified or well-read than you, if you begin to think of yourself as "just" a receptionist, or "just" a junior doctor or "just" a salesperson, you fall into the overwhelmingly large group of people who normalise their lack of potential through the use of limiting language. Through your own behaviour and perception of your current ability and capacity, you are helping to ensure you remain little more than "just" a human being - somewhat ironically with extraordinary potential. People often don't believe that they are capable of anything more than what they currently do because they are in a comfort zone of repetitive behaviours, continuing to do the same things, with little consideration given to what they could do. We focus on here and now and not on where we could go; what we could do. Many people I speak to about this concept of self-limiting potential have never thought about it before. Now that's not necessarily a bad thing, but it is the most significant barrier if you ever want to achieve anything extraordinary, which so many people are oblivious to. So, for the past few years I've been following up the response to my question with: "you are ten thousand times more important than you think you are right now." I can't quantify that of course and that's partly why I say it with so much confidence because no one is able to challenge me on it, however, it gets people thinking and sets a sensational measure of improvement that raises the question of just how much they could push themselves to achieve. In itself, the exercise encourages people to think of the things or ways that they could do things or think differently to produce better results.

Responses to questions I've asked people, such as: "why do you do it this way?" or "what do you think defines an extraordinary person?" have genuinely astounded me. Once after I had presented to a group of researchers and medical scientists, I was asked to sign some copies of my book. Stood in the surprisingly modern space of the Royal College of Physicians in Euston, London, I asked a very intelligent and articulate research professor, as she handed me her copy of my book, what she felt defined an extraordinary person and she said, with all seriousness: "I suppose a superhero or someone with superhuman powers... but then having said that, some of Michelangelo's works are quite extraordinary." Now, some people don't entirely understand what extraordinary means - I mean, do you? Within the context of the question it can appear as though I'm fishing for an especially interesting or unusual answer. So I asked the professor how she would define extraordinary. She said: "I think something that is truly exceptional, far from the norm and out of the reach of most of us." Presumably, if I asked nearly anyone walking down a busy high street at quarter to two in the afternoon if they felt that the word extraordinary summed up a single parent who had been involved in some of the most ground breaking research into cancer treatment, had numerous articles and papers published in scientific publications, written best-selling books under a pseudonym and who was humble only through a seeming ignorance of the impact of her very existence, I think nearly everyone would say that professor was extraordinary. However, the very existence of this book and the *Be a Purple Banana* principle is the fact that however you define extraordinary, either it's "far from the norm," "out of the reach of most of us," "truly exceptional," or, as the Oxford English Dictionary defines it: "very unusual or remarkable," it is, surely, subjective? You may well disagree with some of the examples of extraordinary people that I have included. That's ok. Their stories just might not be read as especially extraordinary to you. Don't let differences in opinion detract from the purpose of the stories though and why I chose to include them - I believe there is much to learn when we start to think just a little differently and question the norm.

Ants

During the last four years I've spent researching the notion of what makes people extraordinary or do extraordinary things, I've asked many questions: What do they think? How are they different from everyone else? When did they realise that they could do things differently? Just what is the difference between ordinary and extraordinary? Can that difference be harnessed? Can it be taught or learnt? After all, each one of us is essentially made of the same stuff: we're all only human. Even if subjectivity rules and what is extraordinary to one person is merely normal to another, there's no denying that individuals like Mahatma Gandhi, Walt Disney, Mother Theresa and Martin Luther-King were extraordinary people, doing something quite remarkable, who have in turn each created lasting legacies and not only made a mark on the world but changed the course of lives for millions upon millions of people. You don't have to agree with or even like the specifics of what they did or the principles of these people - they are undeniably extraordinary. However, this book isn't about changing the world - per se. But it could be if you wanted it to be, if that's what the result of you being extraordinary will be. Some people will argue that these are sensational examples and that you only picked this book up with the intention of being a better salesperson, to satisfy your addiction to self-help books, to be or a more effective teacher, to learn allied business skills - or to feed your penchant for unusual fruit - and now you're being funnelled into starting a revolution. But one of the truly inspiring things that I've discovered over the past four years of researching the difference between ordinary and extraordinary is that many people argue that they aren't the type of person that could be extraordinary or do extraordinary things or that it simply isn't possible to learn to be extraordinary - it's a gift or ability that people are born with. Well, as you'll see, that statement couldn't be further from the truth. There are exceptions to the rule, usually as a result of interference with foetal development or trauma during birth or the critical developmental period, however, on the whole I don't believe that people are born with a natural ability to be extraordinary or do things differently. Even though behaviour is a combination of nature and nurture and cannot exist exclusively of one or the other because of the huge influence of genetics, which cannot be changed, the impact of one's environment and the way in which we are nurtured through key development phases in our lives, has a tumultuous impact on what we believe we can achieve and what we actually do. The ability to think or do something extraordinary is learnt and nurtured. Thankfully though, although parents, guardians and teachers have a lot of responsibility, which is why I really hope many parents and teachers find a copy of this book or that perhaps you buy or lend them a copy, we can nurture this ability ourselves. That is the real purpose of this book: to show you that you really can be extraordinary and to consider the impact this could have on your life and on those around you, for a better world and for you, a more fulfilling life.

A common theme of the people I studied, interviewed and learnt from, who had all achieved extraordinary things in their lives - and many who continue to do so - was that they think and are motivated in ways quite different to most people. I'll reveal exactly what those differences are and how to adopt them. The problem is that ordinary is more often than not more than acceptable: things get done; children learn and sales are made without anything more than ordinary experiences or inputs. But those experiences are forgotten - nothing stands out about them. It's the extraordinary experiences and the extraordinary people that make the biggest impact and differences - these are the people that stand out; that are the most successful. Why are the likes of Walt Disney, Richard Branson, Paul Potts, Sir Ken Robinson, Charlie Chaplin and Mahatma Gandhi so famous, revered and praised? Why are their actions and legacies so memorable? Certainly not because they thought average thoughts, produced ordinary work and let life guide them. Ordinary is taken; it's time to be different and be extraordinary.

For many, being extraordinary is a way of coping with the world. Perhaps a lonely childhood drives them to do things that make them stand out and in turn attract attention and gain popularity. Or being constantly told that they couldn't do something or weren't clever enough unintentionally empowered them to prove that they could indeed do things they had their heart set on. I didn't have a bad start in life; we weren't especially well off as a family but I had a comfortable upbringing. I'm an only child, so benefited from being the single child recipient of attention and gifts and got to enjoy regular holidays. However, I did feel particularly lonely as a child. I wasn't actually very confident socially, which may surprise people who have seen me lecture and experienced me clambering across the backs of chairs in an audience to reach someone to interview, or introducing an eight foot balloon into the room. I'm actually still not especially comfortable in social situations and when I'm not working, really do enjoy my own company and immersing myself in every second of life. But I suppose it could have easily been drugs or alcohol abuse instead, which are the two most common outlets that humans turn to in an attempt to cope. Physical and sexual abuse comes in a close third. Fortunately, instead of indulging in excessive amounts of lurid substances, I saw the amazing potential of people and life.

I suffered with fairly regular transient bouts of depression through my mid-teens and well into my late twenties, which at the time I was relatively confident were all just part of growing up. Not that this understanding made it any easier. Those dark moments of loneliness, anxiety, sleeplessness and struggling to come to terms with the emotional pain I experienced were somewhat numbed and distracted by listening to music to get myself to sleep. However, it is these very experiences that cause so many people to drink or take drugs to escape the pain and that quickly develops into a very dangerous coping mechanism. I often wonder why I didn't turn to those things; what made me choose ants, trees and sunsets instead of smack and cheap cider? Retrospectively, seeing what these addictions have done to the likes of the hugely talented Amy Winehouse and hearing of Russell Brand's own similar experiences, I'm certainly thankful I avoided that. I grew up in the countryside and where some find it fantastically lonely, I have always found it more than beautiful. Walking my dogs across fields was a welcome escape from reality and it still serves as great thinking and quiet time. I remember the first time I experienced my first real high in life. I was about fourteen and shopping in the local town, stood by the clock tower and as I looked down, I noticed a few ants, speedily scurrying around. One of them was carrying a piece of a leaf and I'd read somewhere that an ant can carry an item up to twenty times its own body weight. Maybe some of them are lazy as I've never seen them with anything heavier than a leaf. Having said that, you don't really ever see a lazy ant do you? They are all doing something. You never see an ant dragging its feet or leaning up against a piece of bark, chewing gum. However, carrying twenty times your own body weight is impressive and certainly way out of my scope of achievements: as I get older I've started grunting and making noises when I lift anything heavier than a pen and every time I get up from a chair. When I go to the gym it sounds like an oral percussion troop followed me in. I don't know how long I watched those little ants but I do know that when I looked up and saw the people, the cars, the tall clock tower and the buildings around them, I was amazed. What an incredible world. These tiny creatures have absolutely no comprehension of us; no idea of how wonderful our world is: the intelligence, the construction, the progress and the history. And they don't need to, either. But I got on a bus home and couldn't stop thinking about the fantastic antithesis of our two worlds. I imagined a film where the camera was tightly focused on the ants that I was watching, scurrying around so quickly, their existence consumed by finding the path home and carrying their leafy dinner - and as it zoomed out you saw the scale of the ant compared to the paving slab it was on, compared to a human, compared to a car, compared to a building, still zooming out as you see a town, a county, an entire continent and finally earth, floating in space. I've never forgotten that amazing, enlightening moment, which for me put life into perspective. How can you not be impressed by the wonderful world that we live in? It's just a shame that all too often humans make bad decisions and create some sensationally bad things. So, instead of preparing a vein, I became fascinated with what are essentially natural wonders and highs.

A Purple Banana

So why the title? What is a purple banana? I feel that I ought to have some enlightening response to that when I tell people the title of my book. They certainly look at me intensely, expecting a dramatically revealing reply. Only, I haven't and as I write this I really feel that I need to find a more succinct way of saying that I have always been tickled by that demonstration of how our cognitive process has to interpret negatives in a conversation in order to understand them. For example, when someone says: "don't think of a red kangaroo," or "don't think of a purple banana," you have to think of them, even though you were told not to, in order to comprehend what it is that you aren't supposed to be thinking of. Those images stand out, they are far from ordinary - in fact they are, quite literally, extraordinary. *Be a Purple Banana* is a positive statement and a visual reminder of just how much you or your efforts can stand out, make a difference and be regarded as extraordinary for other people, if you apply the principle of being extraordinary.

My fascination with the extraordinary is today, however, a real addiction. I live for creating extraordinary moments; for making an impact out of the ordinary and for encouraging others that we all have the potential, granted all-be-it sometimes untapped, to be extraordinary, too. Whether at work, in your organisation or in your own personal life, I've written this book to share with you some remarkable techniques and the very principles that help make extraordinary things happen. Resources that will help you become a better salesperson and sell more; that will help you understand how to be more successful in whatever area you choose, whether it be business, baking or indeed life; to show you how to enjoy life and open your eyes to the wonder around you; to be a more effective teacher or to simply take whatever you currently do, or whoever you currently are, out of the restraints of ordinary and make the step-change to achieve something altogether extraordinary. These principles have worked for me - and continue to do so - and for the probably hundreds of thousands of people I have taught them to and I know they will for you, too.

Jez Rose
Buckinghamshire, England. 2015
#BeExtraordinary

FOREWORD

Jez is an expert in human behaviour and more specifically in how to get people to change their behaviour for the better, whilst understanding why we do the things we do. I know what it's like to have little available time when you are focused on driving your own higher performance and achieving goals and Jez does this not only for himself but for organisations and individuals including celebrities and nobility, all over the world.

Be a Purple Banana is at times hilarious but the message is a useful one and for some, it may well be the awakening they need to achieve great things at work or indeed in their personal life. Whatever your reason for reading this, I suggest you begin by embracing the challenges that stand in your way - there's absolutely no point in crying over spilt milk; it's happened. It's done. I share Jez's belief that every human being is capable of achieving extraordinary things, if only we understand that the key is to learn from our perceived failures - and then keep going.

Sir Ranulph Fiennes
"The world's greatest living explorer"
[The Guinness Book of Records]
and recipient of multiple
awards and honorariums.

PREFACE

For many years I conducted corporate seminars where I successfully demonstrated that people have a much better memory than they realised. Mentally and physically you can achieve so much more than you have ever dreamed of - your limitations exist only in your own mind. The concept that "you are much better than you think you are," has always been the foundation of my philosophy.

We are all creatures of habit and have been programmed to think that we cannot be changed. Well, you can – but you need an open mind to receive and then act on, the kind of information that is given in this book.

So, please allow yourself to absorb, think and accept these positive ideas - you will be amazed at the results. Get to know this "new" you, and you will have found a new best friend for the rest of your life

My motto, both in my career and my personal life has always been "Nothing is Impossible." Now this can also apply to your life.

David Berglas
Master Fellowship of
The Academy of Magical Arts,
Hollywood.

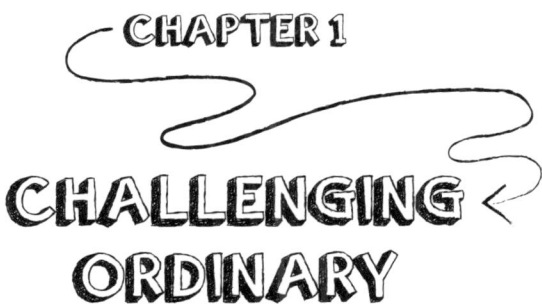

CHAPTER 1

CHALLENGING ORDINARY

"Happiness is a state of mind; it's just according to the way you look at things."

Walt Disney, animator, businessman, producer, director and loved the world over as the father of Mickey Mouse.

Extraordinary is Just a State of Mind

What is it that makes someone extraordinary? Is it their abilities? Or their talent? Or simply their smile? Walt Disney was right you know; the difference between those who stand in the winner's circle and the also-rans, is really quite tiny. Sure there are differences in the way they do things; for example the difference between a winning runner and the one who comes second is probably a few kilojoules of energy. Those few kilojoules may well be the result of a few hours extra training over the course of many months, however, the key difference is their attitude, their mindset and like everything in life, our perspective on things determines our response, our actions and ultimately the consequences of those actions and responses - or inaction, of course.

On the windowsill of my office sits a glass ornament with Walt Disney's quotation about happiness engraved in it. For someone who spends his life traveling the world speaking to and training large groups of people, with lots of performance elements to make learning engaging and fun (the fallout of working as a comedy performer for several years), I've ironically always been one of those "no drama" kinds of people. If someone knocks over a glass and it breaks, or the dog chews a table leg, my first reaction is normally practical: did anyone get hurt? That's probably the result of having lived with a paramedic for so long and a background working in hospital. Does what happened affect anything immediately? Can we clear it up now? Much of life is not permanent, so if it's replaceable - well, it's replaceable. If no one died as a result of something happening, then the result can only be much better than the worst case scenario. That's the bench mark I use for nearly everything: did anyone die? Every moment you are living, somewhere in the world a family are gathered around a loved one, watching their life slowly ebb away; medical professionals are fighting to stem a bleed or otherwise save the life of someone as a result of injury; tears stream down the uncontrollably pained faces of family and friends at a funeral. It is sobering to put things into perspective because, quite often, we don't. We become all consumed with us and what we're doing right now. Our moods and sometimes our entire days are affected by the impact something has on us. Of course, it doesn't make the things that do happen any less serious: a client is unhappy with what you produce, the cat is unwell or the car is badly damaged in the car park - these are far from positive things, however, we have a choice as to how we respond to these. Crying, becoming irate and allowing yourself to be engulfed by stress is simply not going to make your client happy, cheer up the cat or fix your car. Feeling despondent or running late? Left something at home? Shrunk your favourite jumper? Scratched the wooden floor? Missed your turning? So? Some people work themselves into a frenzy; their stress levels rise; they are in a foul mood for the entire day and spend the rest of it slamming things down and sighing a lot. As a result, those around you become irritated and in no time at all you have an oppressive and negative environment, which one person unnecessarily caused because of the way they allowed themselves to be affected by something out of their control. You might know someone who is just like that. It might even be you. If it is you, you might well find that reading this book changes that and offers you a much more balanced and stress-free life, with a new or renewed perspective on your actions and their consequences. Some may say that would be quite extraordinary in itself! The most significant barrier to making the shift from ordinary to extraordinary, in whatever endeavour you wish to do so, is you because no one else can do it for you. Just as you've seen prior to reading this book, all of the possibilities you've had and the opportunities you've turned down up until now were because of your mindset. We've all been in the position where we didn't believe that we could do something or thought it would be too difficult or we were incapable, so passed up the opportunity.

When I decided to write a book about "being extraordinary," I fully expected there to be resistance. After all, if your life will continue and your organisation will carry on, without the need to try or do anything different at all, why rock the boat? Why make any changes? Surely life is there to be lived? Well, these are valid points. Change isn't for everyone and some people are perfectly happy with their life the way it is. However, this book isn't for them and if you're reading this, I imagine you fall into one of two categories of people. You are either seeking something more from one or more aspects of your life, or you are quite happy with things in your life but have an open mind and are one of those "glass half full" people who is happy to consider or reflect on any improvement that may bring further happiness or a sense of fulfilment. It's the existence of the latter, the people like you, why this book has been written.

Let's take you as an example first, as you're most important. This book is not a self-help book and it's not a motivational book, nor is it a life coaching book; it doesn't introduce a unique, secret system to attract wealth that lay uncovered for centuries in a dusty book hidden in a forgotten corner of Kansas. Neither am I going to harp on about how I climbed Everest and how it has so many useful lessons in life (I haven't climbed Everest - I've got asthma). It's not a cheesy pseudo-psychology book and I won't be revealing any three-letter acronyms for reforming your life. I hope more of you are sighing a sigh of relief right now. Instead, this book is about you. More specifically, it's about your brain and your behaviour. In many ways it is like the manual for the human brain that you never got. It may even show you how you can get to where you want to be. If you don't know where you want to be, you may well find you're a lot clearer on that by the end. However, that would be because of the effect of what I have written about and is not my intention with this book. Although if you do have a big revelation at the end and feel fantastic for it, I'll happily take some of the credit for it. It doesn't matter if you're reading this in hope of finding information to help you become a more effective leader; a better teacher; a happier person; a kinder person; to generate wealth or simply because you'd seen me on television or on stage and wanted to find out more about my 'Be Extraordinary' philosophy.

A Journey

Be a Purple Banana is a journey. How many days have you spent working away at your desk until late at night, neglecting your spouse, your pets or your children? How often have you sat watching television when family or friends have gone uncalled? How many "just this one" moments have you had with food and drink that left you overweight and unhappy? Indeed we take for granted the very fact that we are alive. Look around you and it is seemingly few people who understand and appreciate just how finite life is; how precious it is. We would all probably admit that we know life is too short for holding grudges and bottling up anger and bitterness, however, we do little about it. Some people appear to grasp life and the opportunities it presents and indeed create their own opportunities. These people aren't abnormal, however, they are, in a sense, extraordinary because it isn't common, it isn't the norm for people to readily make the most of every day or work to a positive solution. It is common, however, for people to focus on a problem, spend time talking about, debating and concentrating on something that has gone wrong, all the time not looking to the future for a solution and to move on. I was talking to my uncle Nigel about this recently and he reiterated my point by stating that his wife and he had been married nearly thirty years but that the time has just zipped by. Here he stood, nearly thirty years on looking back at just how quickly the time goes. And none of that time we get back. None of those people lost will we ever see again. Every second that ticks away; every minute that passes us by; every hour that escapes us and every day that disappears - every Christmas that "came around so quickly" is full of both potential memories and opportunities for us to create extraordinary moments for ourselves and those around us. Every single day. But isn't it sad that we have to stand gathered around a loved one's grave to be reminded of this? To be touched with that guilt of just how many opportunities we've neglected and to grow old unfulfilled, unhappy and grieving for the person we dreamed of being but didn't grow into. I can't think of anything worse.

Just how our own choices about health or time spent can impact not only ourselves but also other people in our family, so too can choices we make about whether we continue to be ordinary or make the leap to extraordinary. Personally I believe that the option to be ordinary has been taken by far too many people, so it's simply not an option for me. And the process begins by asking three questions to nearly everything I do, before I make a decision:

Why?

Why does it have to be done this way? This question helps push yourself to find new ways of doing things; searching to improve and challenge the status quo. Quite often you find that the only reason things are done the way they are, is because "they've always been done that way." This answer, combined with a resistance to change is crippling for productivity and will prevent any movement towards creating anything extraordinary. How will anything extraordinary come about if you keep doing things the same way? By repeating the same actions the same way you'll only ever get the same result. Looking at things from a different point of view is the cornerstone of creating anything extraordinary.

How?

How can we make this better? Striving to always improve what you are doing, to find a more efficacious way of doing things is the best kick-start to actually doing it. Many of us are gold-star procrastinators and put everything off until the time is right. Only the time never is. In my experience, that time never comes but this cautious mindset is that of pretty much every ordinary person I've ever met.

What?

What would Grandma do? Now, obviously, you don't know my Grandma - and more's the pity. But you can ask the same question about anyone else that you respect for making sound judgements and good decisions, to help guide you. My Grandma is not a Saint, nor is she perfect all the time. But everything she does has humanity at its heart and a genuine desire to do the very best. That's a fantastic role model to have and offers you a different perspective to whatever you're doing.

There's also a lot to be said for not accepting the ordinary, which is what makes the "why?" question so useful. By not accepting what has gone before, you open up your mind to many alternatives that were previously invisible to you. If for whatever reason, there is in fact no way to improve what you have been doing or the way you have been doing it, you can still ask yourself how you could do it differently - there's always something that can be changed for the better, even if it's simply by introducing a random act of kindness. They never cease to inspire me and I've included just a small selection of some of my favourites in the hope that they inspire you, too. I find that sometimes in life, all it takes is someone else to do something, which puts you in a position where you find yourself asking: "why didn't I do that?" or "could I do that?" Those moments that make you pause just for a moment and think, happen all too infrequently in the rat race most of us are caught up in.

Random Acts

Syed Muzamil Hasan Zaidi did not spend his twenty first Birthday partying hard or lying semi-conscious on a high street, covered in his own vomit with his pants around his ankles, talking to a pigeon. Instead, this dynamic twenty one year old carried out twenty one random acts of kindness. He wrote letters to policemen, thanking them for all they do; bought ice cream for all of the military guards sitting in the heat; bought bottles of water for policemen and gardeners, cleaned dirty windscreens for free for an hour; planted a tree; cleaned a random person's car in a car park; had a heart to heart conversation with the cleaner at a coffee shop; conducted barrier duties at a border while the guards had dinner; wrote appreciation letters to instructors for choosing education over corporate jobs; cleaned up rubbish on his university campus; distributed tissue serviettes to people in a cafe; printed happy leaflets and distributed them in the university and at intersections; gave juice cartons to young children walking the streets in the heat; gave way to anyone on the road; gave apples out to labourers who couldn't find jobs; gave a lift to hostel students from university so that they didn't have to walk home; distributed yellow roses and happy leaflets to nurses at the local hospital; helped a taxi driver at the roadside; gave the staff at a restaurant sweets because they didn't get a day off on Eid; gave his parents a special hug for being the best parents on the planet and bought a twelve year old homeless boy ice-cream and chips after he said he liked them. Finally, he distributed balloons at a local orphanage.

Syed's story reminded me of a photo I saw doing the rounds on the internet. It shows a disabled man, with no legs, laying in the middle of a street. It looks like it may be India. The rain is pouring down and the man is clearly struggling. Where others in the background of the image were walking by, one woman is seen holding an umbrella over the man, shielding him from the heavy down pour. She herself exposed to the rain.

So impressed was I by these random acts of kindness by complete strangers, that I made a compilation video and put it on YouTube. The video shows another image I found of a teenage girl in a country that looks like it could be African. She has no shoes and appears upset. She is wiping tears from her face. A white man who appears to be a tourist, has removed his flop flops and is offering them to her. Another photo shows a restaurant receipt. The total is 32.32, however, in the tip section, someone has written 50.00, making a total of 82.32. A little note on the edge of the receipt explains it. It reads: "A random act of love in memory our son, Joel. He brightened everyone's day. May this brighten yours. Thank you." [sic]. The video has been viewed more than 5,000 times, which you could deduce hints that there is a fair amount of interest in random acts of kindness. You can see it for yourself at this link: http://bit.ly/bapbkindness

In each of these cases, others simply walked on by, or watched on. But one person did something different; they didn't accept what was ordinary about the situation. They became extraordinary by being the difference for someone else. No Nobel Prize or reams of published articles balanced on a cluttered office book shelf. No super powers. Nothing extraordinary about them to look at if you passed them by in the street. And that person could be you. That is just one of the many things I have found so fascinating about this concept of what being extraordinary means. In practice it actually means so many different things to different people but one thing remains consistent: the need to buck a trend; to think in such a way that isn't what is considered normal, or what the majority are doing. When we think about doing something that doesn't perhaps follow suit, that isn't what others would say is what is typically, usually - or normally - done, very often people assume it must be rebellious or go against the grain in some way. However, that simply doesn't hold water.

Only 10%?

It is, however, very easy to read these acts of people behaving in an extraordinary way and reflect from the comfort of your chair (I'm assuming you're sitting down; standing up while reading always looks so uncomfortable), that you would have done the same. But keep searching; keep asking yourself if that is really true or simply an ideal reflection of your perception of your own character. Although some of you will indeed be that person, many of you will be surprised that you're not the extraordinary person you might have hoped that you were. There is an ancient parable attributed to the Cherokee Indians, which goes something like this, from memory: a young Cherokee man is hauled before the tribe's elders, who are concerned about his aggressive tendencies. One of the elders takes the young man to one side and tells him that his anger is in fact understandable, for all humans have within them two wolves. One wolf is generous, humble and has an open heart. The other is aggressive, arrogant and selfish. The wolves are in constant battle with one another because neither is powerful enough to destroy the other. So his aggressiveness is only natural. The young man turns to the elder and asks: "but which wolf will win?," to which the elder replies: "the one you feed."

Much in your own life is up to you; our future and life path is carved out as a result of the choices and decisions we make on a moment by moment basis. Do you want to get out of bed today? Do you want to eat a large, fattening burger? Will you donate some of your monthly pay to charity? Will you stop and think of ways in which you can do things differently? Will you continue to work late, narrowing the time you spend with your friends and family? Will you allow yourself to get angry and consumed with negative emotions, or stop and do something about the problems? Will you take the motorway home, or the scenic route? The decisions we make on a daily basis determine which wolf grows. Thomas Edison is just as famous for inventing the first commercially viable incandescent lamp as he is for many of his eloquent thoughts: "If we did all the things we were capable of doing, we would astound ourselves." It is often said that our brains only ever perform at ten percent of our overall capacity. I'm not sure how anyone would be able to quantify or qualify that and I've not seen any evidence to support such a dramatic statement either. Personally, I think that's a fairly ludicrous statement to make given the advances there have been in neuroscience. Perhaps someone said that a long, long time ago when little was known about the brain and it has stuck. However, my own experience based on ten years of training people for high performance and working with them to get the best out of themselves and the people they work with, along with the many examples of individuals, groups and organisations I've witnessed achieving truly extraordinary things, is that we choose not to do many of the things we are capable of doing. We choose the easy route; the less complicated route and the less risky option.

If you think ordinary thoughts, ordinary is all you will ever achieve. Like much in life; it begins and ends with you. Your journey to unleashing extraordinary potential, which I believe is already locked away inside of you, has already begun. As you read my ramblings, it is my intention that you'll begin to make extraordinary changes to not only your way of thinking and approaching things, but to whatever and wherever you apply the strategies, principles and techniques, whether that be home, work or your personal life. The results will, I hope, be extraordinary. Which I suppose is obvious to you now, however, what I have learned is that, generally, extraordinary results often have an extraordinary impact.

Contemplating Life

Brittany Maynard is 29. She's recently just moved from San Francisco to Oregon and she's beautiful. Really very beautiful. She's also newly-wed. Young, beautiful and just married sounds very much like a fairytale. Especially when you add to that Brittany's plans to go travelling, mountain climbing with friends and to start a family. She's a perfect example of extraordinary thinking and extraordinary action because Brittany has terminal brain cancer and today as I type, only has seventeen days left to live. The reason Brittany recently moved was not to start up a marital or family home but because Oregon is one of only five states in the USA where dignified death is not illegal: on the 1st November 2014, Brittany will take a prescribed pill that will end her life. A choice she made as an alternative to increasing pain, seizures and growing weakness, letting her condition slowly and painfully kill her.

Persistent headaches resulted in Brittany seeking help from her doctor. Scans of her head showed an aggressive malignant tumour on her brain and it was suggested she may have just five to ten years left to live. However, in April 2014, her condition had worsened and she was then diagnosed with a stage four glioblastoma and advised it was likely that she only had just six months left to live. It was at this point, with so little time left and having been educated as to how debilitating her brain tumour would be, Brittany chose to consciously end her life without pain and suffering. Interestingly,

I read in the news that she has spoken publicly about how her decision to die is not a suicide. She said: "I want to live. I wish there was a cure for my disease but there's not."

You may wonder why Brittany has chosen the 1st November 2014 to end her life. Her husband's birthday is on October 30th and she wants to spend one more special occasion with him. By the time you read this, knowing that its publication is due early 2015, Brittany Maynard will no longer be alive and because she understood just how early her life was ending, she set up a fund for people to donate in her memory, to help other people in a similar situation to hers. The gesture may sound familiar, especially for those of you reading this in the UK. I've just navigated to the Just Giving page of nineteen year old Stephen Sutton. He had a lofty target of raising one million pounds for the Teenage Cancer Trust. So far, his donations page indicates that he achieved 448% of his target and it's increasing every day. The Teenage Cancer Trust have benefited from almost four and a half million pounds, from one boy's efforts and for not accepting to fulfil an ordinary life. Similar to Brittany, when Stephen learnt that his cancer was incurable, he dedicated the rest of his life to raising funds for charity and as a result he directly enabled two million, nine hundred thousand pounds to be invested in eight specialist cancer units across England; one million, two hundred thousand pounds to support vital research and train professionals who work with young people with cancer; half a million pounds to enhance access to information for young people and two hundred thousand pounds will directly help fifteen hundred patients attend information events over the next five years. However, Stephen didn't just raise money; he wrote a bucket list and achieved some extraordinary things, which included of course raising more than one million pounds for charity; a skydive; writing a book; organise a flash mob; fly first class and perhaps the most poignant addition to Stephen's bucket list was this: "42) Inspire someone else to become a doctor or fundraiser." When I read that line, it reminded me why hearing examples of other people's extraordinary efforts, ways of thinking and feats was so important because it's not only about us; it's about remembering how our actions can impact others, too.

CHAPTER 2

EXTRAORDINARY EXAMPLES

"A child takes something apart, breaks it up in order to know it; to force its secret. The cruelty itself is motivated by something deeper – the wish to know the secret of things and life"

Erich Fromm, German social psychologist, psychoanalyst, sociologist, humanist and philosopher.

Up!

My good friend, Dr. Ian Dunbar, is the world's most eminent animal behaviourist. He helped launch and popularise the notion of training puppies, thirty one years ago, prior to which such a thing was unheard of. It's almost inconceivable to think now that puppy training didn't exist. Obviously at some point it didn't exist; I've no doubt Plato had more than enough on his plate without considering if he should train his puppy. I'm presuming of course he had a puppy but am well aware that it is most likely that he did not. Yet to think that just thirty one years ago, all of those draughty village halls and veterinary waiting rooms were not being used to their full potential.

Through this and other endeavours, Ian completely revolutionised pet dog training, largely by using food lures, instead of force. It was very common-place for dogs to be shown that what they were doing was wrong by beating them with a rolled up newspaper or squirting lemon juice in their face, or by forcibly taking a hand to their body. Until Ian suggested that perhaps we could just ask them to do an alternative behaviour that you can reward them for, contingent on them stopping the problem behaviour. So, for example, if your dog is jumping up at people, you would ask him to "sit." If he's sitting, he's not jumping up. Then you can give him a reward for sitting. Almost poetically simple isn't it? Ian worked tirelessly to teach dog owners how dogs learn and that rubbing a dog's nose in its urine when it soils in the house, is actually likely to make the problem worse because the dog learns to do it when you're not around, in an attempt to avoid the punishment. Whereas, when we understand that the only reason the dog goes to the toilet in the house is because they like absorbent substances to pee on, we've got not just an understanding of why they do these things but a perfect solution: provide them with a piece of turf by the back door, in a litter tray, that they can go on, which they'll then associate with when you let them outside. No other single person has done as much for pet dog training as Ian and it is both fascinating and entertaining to listen to him speak, reflecting on his forty years' experience in the field. He spends his time now lecturing to dog trainers worldwide, however, every now and again he is called upon to do something a little different, like speak at the TED conference in

Los Angeles in 2007 and advise the Pixar team on how to bring Dug the dog to life most realistically and comically, in the animated hit, *Up!*

One of Ian's many legacies is as a result of something that his Grandfather taught him: that to touch an animal is an earned privilege, not a human right. It is this early lesson that has shaped his force-free methods and techniques, using basic learning theory and applied psychology to create a remarkably efficacious and efficient way of training pet dogs. On his Grandfather's farm, Ian would be encouraged as a child to handle the young cows, feed them by hand and spend time around them. His Grandfather's theory was that if the cows were introduced to children at a young and impressionable age, during a key period of developmental critical socialisation, they would not be scared of children and therefore, be safer to be around. Reflecting on this, Ian realised that this was a key technique in socialising animals to people that was not taken advantage of. Subsequently, he spent much of his career educating on the importance of the early socialisation of pet dogs, to prevent common temperament and behaviour problems.

Dogged Determination

The impact Ian has had on society over the past thirty years is hugely underestimated. There are an estimated eight and a half million dogs in the United Kingdom alone. Today, thousands of dog trainers, veterinarians and dog professionals flock to see him speak, however, when he first presented his ideas and techniques, which today seem obvious and are almost universally accepted and indeed have created careers for others who have built on them, he was ridiculed and regularly turned up to lectures to which not a single other person turned up. Despite evidence acquired through research he conducted while researching dog behaviour at the University of California, Berkeley, many people were vocal that his methods simply wouldn't work. Not that they tried or tested them of course, they were just vocal about their uninformed opinions. After all, for as long as anyone could remember, dogs were pulled, pushed, hit, forced into position and punished. Ian's insights into dog behaviour are thought-provoking: "The dog doesn't understand English - or French or Swahili for that matter. If you've not taught the dog what the rules are, how can you punish him for breaking them?" And so it is for humans, too. At its most basic level, learning theory tells us that if you want to see more of a behaviour, you reinforce or reward it. If you want to see less of a behaviour, you punish it - which, sadly, is normally the first reaction of most humans: punish using punitive physical force, shouting or what is essential psychological bullying, in the form of belittling, for example. But punishment is less effective as a strategy to change behaviour in the long-term than reinforcement. Positive reinforcement is the most effective form of behaviour control we know. Ian struggled to encourage people to change and there are still people today that do not appear to understand these extremely simple concepts. These concepts of behaviour change are so strikingly simple to explain and so widely documented and proven, that their blind ignorance is most likely due to a resistance to be proven wrong. That is a really troubling human trait, which prevents much progress and harmony in the human race. However, Ian didn't give up. He let the ridiculing and obstructions go over his head, pushing forwards with what he knew deep down was right. Instead of responding to the doubters and the neighsayers, he used his energy and efforts to publish and promote his work, research and highlight methods he knew would make owning a dog easier and more enjoyable for owners and kinder and more fun for dogs.

He believed in his work and in his vision of taking dog ownership from wartime punishment-based methods of forced learning, to fair and effective. Ian's story is something of a one man revolution and if you or anyone you know has used food to train dogs, it's thanks to Ian's work popularising this method. No dramatic international press releases; no advertising campaigns and no hit television show (and more's the pity). Just one man and a life-long quest to do what he felt he knew, and proved scientifically, was correct. It's a useful reminder of the maxim that Walt Disney made famous: "always believe in a thing and never give up."

It Begins and Ends

The notion of being extraordinary is one very close to my heart. As I write this I receive news that my Grandma, who has dementia and was moved into a home about six months ago (a decision I was never supportive of, protesting my evidence that it was likely to make her worse

- it did), probably doesn't have long left to live. She's not eating and is drinking very little; simply sat in a chair, her life ebbing away. It is most likely that nearly every person reading this book will have experienced the tragic loss of a loved one and will be able to relate somewhat to my pain. However, my Grandma really was someone quite special. I know everyone says that, but she really was. She was born on 22nd December 1926 in Melbourn, Cambridgeshire, where she spent most of her youth. The job we, her family, know the most about is during the war when she worked as a nurse auxiliary, looking after children. She adores children and always has done.

On her sixtieth birthday, she thought nothing of parachuting out of a plane; the enlarged photograph of her standing in a ploughed field in front of a crumpled parachute, beaming with that trademark twinkle in her eyes and rosy cheeks, hung with pride on the wall by the stairs in their home. On a few occasions she had to stay in hospital; for a new hip and after a fall - the usual when you're over fifty. If you're approaching or around fifty, this book will serve many educational purposes for you, especially. However, something quite extraordinary happened on more than one occasion when she was hospitalised. She received thank you cards when she left - from the hospital staff. She literally lit up a room with her smile, twinkling eyes and laughter. She talked to anyone and everyone - much to the irritation of my Grandad. Beautiful in her youth and right through into her elderly years, she was of the generation that had really charming qualities that we seem to have lost today: dressed impeccably whenever she went out and wonderfully polite to anyone that would stop to chat with her. My Grandad used to have to sometimes literally drag her away! As the second grandchild of the family and within just a thirty minute drive of my Grandparents' home, I was doted on with baking, camp-building in the dining room, which involved moving the furniture and draping bed sheets and blankets over the chairs; playing at being a shopkeeper in the garden using the low wall as a counter and having access to a huge box of Lego. Grandma had a heart and spirit that many would say was saintly and an energy and youthfulness that masked her true years. Grandma would not sit still, literally - she was always on the go, with the exception of eating, playing the piano or the odd "forty winks." She had no favourite chair as so many older people do. What am I saying, I have a favourite chair and I'm not old. As soon as she woke up she would be up and doing something: cleaning, baking, mending, gardening, washing. Always something. In recent years she was given a walking frame to help her with her balance. Getting her to use it slowly and not push it around so quickly was a constant battle, her mind always one step ahead of her body. She thought of it as getting in her way and slowing her down but watching her with it and the speed she used to go, reminded me of that time my friend and I were at the dog race track and he got his shoelace stuck in the electric hare. Some things just take off.

I remember clearly the first couple of years of her dementia setting in; not that back then we thought it was anything more than a few transient moments of old age forgetfulness. But, oh, we laughed about it! That wicked sense of humour, tear-inducing laughter and ability to find the positive in everything: "what's your name again?" would bring a good five minutes of fun that our sides would hurt and we'd have to try our hardest not to inflict any more laughter pains! But the memory lapses and confusion gradually got worse and the first time I knew it was serious and had gone past the point of no return was when I went to visit her in their bungalow in Dereham in Norfolk. I walked into the front room to see her, sat in a chair (which is where you now always see her). It was like a train had hit me right in the chest. I can't describe the instantaneous, hard realisation that hit me. The sparkle in her eyes had gone. They were dull. She looked overweight, grey and spent much of my visit being nasty, rude and obstructive. I cried for most of the two and a half hour journey home. That visit and subsequent time spent thinking about her made me realise how important our minds are. That sensational organ tucked away deep within our protective skull, which we give so little thought to, will create the difference between ordinary and extraordinary. After all, what do we have without our mind? Who are we without our mind? What is the point in having health and a body that works if you can't enjoy it, understand it or even comprehend it? Our character traits, the choices we make, our beliefs, desires, passions, our preferences, our foibles - our hopes and dreams, are all rooted in our mind. It's a sad reality that those things we cannot see, we tend to forget about, which is just the very issue social lobbyists have about so-called invisible disabilities. Dementia is a cruel and devastating illness that slowly strips away sufferers, causing torment and suffering to family, friends and those around them. And although she isn't physically dead and I don't think of her as so, my Grandma, the Grandma I knew and loved so dearly, has been gone for some time now. I haven't visited for a while. I'm not keeping track of the days but I know it has been longer than I would normally leave it: it's not enjoyable for me and she doesn't appear to remember much of who I am, which probably hurts more than any alternative. The favourite grandchild, with so many happy memories that now seem to pale into insignificance because the person you shared them with and who created them for you, appears to have turned their back on them - and you. Now of course I know that isn't for a second the real truth and she doesn't know what she's doing - much of the time she doesn't fully comprehend where she is or why she is there. The extraordinary woman I once knew has gone. And you will have to trust me when I tell you that the world is worse off without her.

But what was it that made my Grandma extraordinary? I have never heard of patients receiving thank you cards from hospital staff before. Her love of people and communicating with others is certainly something you don't see much of. People often think I'm odd for striking up a conversation with the person serving me behind the bar, or while waiting in a queue. How often do you walk past people even in the street you live, without acknowledging them or having any form of conversation? However, for the individual concerned, you can see that they relish the interaction. Their face lights up, they smile and they actively engage in conversation and witty banter with you. More often than not they'll tell me that I made their day. Really? By simply talking to them? I didn't tell them I was a secret millionaire and write a big fat cheque out, or introduce Carole Smiley as she jumped out from behind a doorway and revealed a complete interior redecoration for them. I just had what probably reads, a rather ordinary conversation with them. Yet the fact that it happened propels it into the extraordinary. It stands out because it's different - it's a moment in their life that, all-be-it for a short time in this example, lingers and has an impact, as it doesn't normally happen. The more I thought about this notion of extraordinary; doing extraordinary things, being an extraordinary person, I came to understand that here is, like most things subject to perception, a scale of extremes. Conversation and making a difference to someone's day is at one end of the imaginary scale and I'd imagine winning a Nobel Prize for saving the world from a deadly infection is at the other. Do you see how easy achieving something extraordinary can be though?

Trousers

Unlike my Grandma, we do have the ability to think in extraordinary ways; to do extraordinary things and to make an extraordinary difference to our lives and the lives of those around us. And it isn't a difficult thing for us to do. I own one pair of jeans, which I don't wear all that often, and quite a few suits, which I wear a lot. However, when I'm not in a suit, the only other trousers I own are Edwardian-styled Vauxhall trousers, which I have tailored by a lady in the North of England who is delightfully trapped in that era. You know how everyone has a "claim to fame," well one of mine is that Monty Don (the gardener and as I type this, one of the presenters of the television programme Gardener's World) wears the same trousers as me. Obviously we have our own pairs but they are made by the same lady. I know it's not really that much of a claim to fame but it is much more tangible than one lady who I met when speaking at a conference in Tenerife, who told me that her claim to fame was that her Mother's, sister's neighbour once cleaned the carpets for Norman Wisdom's Mother. Anyway, if you are having trouble picturing my trousers and what I look like normally, they are the straight legged trousers that sit high up above your waist band, with the tall, fish-tail shaped back and held up with traditional buttoned braces (or suspenders for our American readers). Why do I wear such outdated trousers? Is it the only thing I can find to accessorise my Edwardian moustache style? I find them incredibly comfortable and I really like the style. That's all. I don't often wear them when working as I prefer a suit so I wear them mostly at home. Inevitably I might need to go out to the shops or post office, for example, which is when something really fascinating happens. People nod and smile at me or they approach me to tell me how much they like my braces or trousers. At first I was pleasantly surprised but when I began my obsession with the extraordinary, all of this trouser attention got me thinking: if my traditional trousers or the fact that I'm wearing braces is something different enough for them to make a point to comment on them, how ordinary must their lives be? Which in itself isn't a problem, of course, but it does mean that there is plenty of scope for introducing extraordinary moments every single day, which can raise a smile, make people pause and reflect and create a difference. One could argue that actually you just don't see that style of fashion often, therefore, in itself it is something out of the ordinary, however, that is just my point. It isn't about the trousers or my fashion choice, it's about choosing to do things that are unexpected and not necessarily what would be considered ordinary.

Who decides what ordinary is anyway? I have never seen any rules or regulations that define what is ordinary. Surely if extraordinary is subjective then by default, ordinary is, too? For Goths, black mascara, lashings of eye-shadow and a healthy dose of safety pins and chains are the name of the game. For Betty Postlethwaite, Chairman and Honorary Treasurer of the village bowls club, sensible flat brown shoes, tweed skirts pleated to within an inch of their life and a cardigan "just in case" are what is normal. Tea in a china cup, with a compulsory saucer and those little fig rolls are normal. Not cheap cider and loud, heavy music, which our Goth friends might well consider normal. Is Betty's perception of normal and ordinary more correct or more worthy than our Goth's interpretation? I am of course being pedantic and the answer is, of course, no, however, it raises an interesting point about the definitions of extraordinary and our individual interpretations of just what makes something, or someone, extraordinary. I will explore this in more detail later in the book. After all, here I am writing a book about what extraordinary is and how you can embrace the principles of being extraordinary, putting them into practice within your organisation, your job, your role or indeed your life, yet so far I am yet to fully address what they might mean to you and perhaps most importantly, what they mean to me, offering you a benchmark.

Beaten

In some respects Oprah Winfrey is one of the most influential women in the world. You may know her as the chat show host from American television, or you may recognise her from her successful business endeavours and philanthropy. Her life achievements are undeniably extraordinary, given her more than humble beginnings. Oprah refers to her childhood as "damaged." She was born into a poor family in Mississippi during the time of racial segregation and was physically abused as a child. She recalls one time as a child when she received what she describes as a "terrible beating." She was dressing to attend Sunday School and as she turned to put on her blouse, she saw a glimpse of her back in the mirror. The whelps from the beating had swollen; some were beginning to scar and others were still bleeding. As Oprah put the blouse on, she recalls being whipped again because the blood had come through the blouse. What is interesting about listening to her speak about her childhood, is that she says she holds no grievances or judgement or anger about it. Although she readily admits that she did for a long time, she reflects with a wise and wonderfully intelligent and practical view that people do only what they know how to do and when they know better they then do better. It just so happens that the period of time and culture in which Oprah grew up, beating children was what people did. It was normal. It was accepted because her parents were beaten and their parents were beaten and their parents before them were also beaten. It's all they knew how to handle children. Oprah explains how even if she did something that was the least inoffensive thing she could do, such as drop a glass or speak out of turn, or play, it could result in being whipped. She recalls a story of when she was returning from the well, bringing water back and playing with the water with her fingers. They were so poor that they had no electricity or plumbing. She returned to the house with the water, which is when her Grandmother told Oprah that she had seen her playing with the water. She was told to put the bucket down and was whipped for playing with the water.

Oprah Winfrey was raped when she was nine years old, which is when a period of sexual abuse began. Her response to this is both inspiring and enlightening: "all of those things that have happened have helped to make me a stronger, more vital woman who can now share those stories in a way I hope lifts somebody else up, to say: 'look at me - I made it, so can you' - and that to me is the whole point about being famous actually." She is candid and clear about how she survived her childhood and talks about how you can survive if there is someone to help you. In Oprah's case it wasn't actually a person who helped her, it was books. The "loneliness and sense of abandonment" she felt as a child, which are the words Oprah uses to describe her childhood, was helped because of her ability to read stories. She had books. Books and the belief that her life would one day get better. If her story was not extraordinary enough, she remembers one day when she was watching from the screen door at the porch at the back of her house, watching her Grandma boiling clothes and hanging them on the line. Her Grandmother said: "you better stand there girl and watch me because you got to learn how to do this." Oprah remembers thinking that she didn't actually have to watch this because there was no way she was going to be boiling clothes and hanging them out to dry. She believed her life was not going to turn out that way. In spite of the whippings delivered by her Grandmother, it was her who instilled in her the belief that she was just as good as anyone else and taught her to read and write. By the time Oprah began Kindergarten, the UK's version of pre-school, she could already read and write. Some years after completing her education, Oprah Winfrey, the little poor girl from Mississippi who began life so broken, got her big break after winning a beauty pageant and securing a position as an anchor for a local television station.

Attention

Have you ever been in that position where you're driving along a road and someone does something incredibly stupid: they overtake on a blind bend on a dark, snowy night or perhaps they cut you up on the motorway, having only just undercut you. Your innate response to this may well be to flash your lights, or sound your horn, to which they respond by slamming on their brakes, or waving their fist at you or giving you the international sign for "I'm perturbed": the middle finger. This lack of acceptance of the consequences created as a result of people's actions is exactly why I enjoy watching police television programmes, for the sheer comedic value of someone hurling obscene abuse at police officers, while protesting their absolute innocence, having been caught red handed climbing out of a ground floor window, with a bag marked "swag." But I digress. Being extraordinary is not about attention seeking, or going against the grain to be rebellious - or even necessarily standing out, per se. It is about considering doing something different to what would be expected in any given situation, with an understanding that the consequence could well change things for the better.

I wholeheartedly agree with Walt Disney's statement that happiness is a state of mind - but so, too, are most emotions. If you can give birth relatively pain-free through meditation or hypnosis and some people are racist and others aren't, surely anything is simply a state of mind, not just happiness? We have a quite remarkable ability, as humans, to control and manipulate our emotional responses, sometimes subconsciously - unique to the mammalian world, as far as we know. Imagine an actor who wakes up late for work. He's flustered and in rushing around to quickly get ready, trips over the cat and twists his ankle. During his frantic showering antics, he gets shampoo is his eye and in the desperate yet temporarily blind attempt to claw it out, knocks his elbow on the tiled wall of the shower. As he's driving to the theatre, he receives a telephone call from his girlfriend, which he takes hands free of course, to inform him that the cat is very unwell and needs to be rushed to the vet and that, while she's there, she's going to end their relationship. He arrives at work and despite all of this, the director requires him to perform to a packed out paying audience, in the role of a happy lottery winner. How does the actor achieve this? How does he behave in such a way that you believe he is the happiest man alive, having just won a huge sum on the lottery when in reality he is having quite possibly the worst day of his life? Good actors and especially method actors, would tell you that they have to feel the emotions of the character they are playing; they become that character and suspend all actual, real emotions of theirs, in order for the performance to be as realistic and convincing as possible. Such is the skill of a good actor. So, it's not that they are performing the part of someone who is in a good mood but that actually they feel awful: quite the opposite. By playing the part of the lottery-winning man, the actor experiences a part of that character's emotions, too, and temporarily suspends their sadness. For a period of time, they don't experience that sadness. It's almost as though they have control of a light switch that enables them to turn on an emotional response via the process of distraction. But actors are not unique in this: we are all capable of changing our mindset; switching our emotional response. You have probably done this yourself, when you need a day off from work, for example. You call into work, making sure that the television and radio are off and the children are strapped in the car ready for their day at Alton Towers. You strain your voice, doing your best to sound upset, bored, unwell and reserved, all at the same time: "Julie? Hi, it's Keith. Do I? Do I sound that bad? Well I feel it to be honest. I don't think I'll be able to make it in today; I just need to go to bed and try to rest. I'm so weak. I had to get Carol to dial the number for me. What's that? No, I don't think it's terminal - probably one of those twenty four hour bug things. I hope. Yes, I'll call you in the morning. So sorry, Julie. Thanks for understanding. Apologise to the team for me will you? I'll make myself a Lemsip and think of them while I'm trying to pull through. Okay, thanks - bye." You put the receiver down, grab your keys and get into the car shouting: "Okay kids, let's go! Who wants to go on the roller coaster first?!"

Of course, I'm not suggesting for a second that you've ever taken dishonest time off from work, however, I'm sure you can relate to my point - hypothetically at least. We have a quite remarkable ability to change our emotional responses to events in our lives. The actions of other people and I believe this resilience of mind is quite possibly one of the most effective qualities that we possess - and it is this adaptable control of our mindset which allows us to shift from the ordinary to the extraordinary. From my experience, many people struggle to change how they think about things. It's usually because whatever their opinion about something, carved out of a certain way of thinking about it or positioning it within their own mind, it has elicited an emotional response within them. People so passionately believe in certain things that they lose the ability to critically rationalise or, even worse, develop an opinion about something which they know little to nothing about, as a result of their emotional response to it. While it does take some conscious effort to change the way you think about something, the key to changing your mindset is firstly to remove perceived barriers and obstructions, which would otherwise prevent you from doing so and in itself, this is one of the key differences between those people who deliver ordinary and extraordinary things: when presented with an obstacle or challenge, they do not give up - they do not perceive the obstacles as problems, simply challenges. If something presents as a problem, it simply raises a question: "what do we need to do in order to achieve this?" This simple philosophy turns any problem or obstruction into a solution, helping to trivialise those things you perceive to be obstructing you. Perhaps, because I questioned everything as a child (I was the one who always asked: "why?"), I have developed an ingrained determination to discover ways to make things happen. If I am told something is not possible or am told the answer is "no," immediately I want to know how we can ale the answer "yes," or what needs to done in order to achieve what we set out to do. That in itself is not an ordinary way of looking at things. Most people, from my experience at least, accept the very first barrier or challenge they are faced with and then begin to qualify the argument for not counting; they'll say things like: "well, it will take too long," or, "it's obviously not meant to be," or even worse: "it's just too much effort." My response is usually: "what do we need to do in order to make this happen?" I know that you are reading this and feeling immense sympathy for my fiancée right now, along with anyone that works with me. I can't say I disagree with you.

When the barriers are very real, however, and we are faced with a more serious or permanent problem, a different question to ask yourself is: "if someone gave me one million pounds to do this, would I do it?" If the answer is "yes," then it's clearly not an obstruction that cannot be overcome; it's just that you either do not want to or will not. I use this 'million pound principle' regularly, to help myself and others get things done that are important. For example, I'm currently learning to speak Spanish more fluently. I have a lesson each week and my Spanish teacher sets me homework to do throughout the week. However, I lead an extremely busy life and always have work I can get on with. The list of creating resources, writing, marketing, managing projects, replying to emails, writing thank you cards, signing books and working, of course, is continually long. Once my Spanish books go back onto the shelf, it is very easy for me to forget about them and I very often subsequently fill ten hours a day with other work or activities that need doing. But no one ever became a better salesperson by buying a book about sales technique that sat on their bookshelf unread. No one, to my knowledge, has ever qualified as a pilot by simply being interested in planes. And so it is that, unless I actually read and learn Spanish by practicing, my knowledge and language skill won't develop at all. But I'm very busy, so I ask myself: "if someone gave me one million pounds to do an hour of Spanish studying today, would I do it?" The answer is "yes" - every time. Then I know that it's a case of me either not being focused enough to do it or simply my Mr Procrastination heavyweight kicking into action again. What I wanted to do in that hour I could actually fit in somewhere else if I was being given one million pounds, which means that it is possible to create the time to do my Spanish study. By the way, if you do happen to be in the position to pay someone one million pounds to study Spanish for an hour, I would like to publicly declare my interest in that position here. It's a really quick process that helps focus your mind. It's the same with my client relationship programme: it takes a lot of effort and time to maintain the relationships with our clients, to the level that I demand but I know that as a result of the contact, my team and I have with my clients, we provide a service and a detail of interaction that is, in most cases, far from ordinary or expected. It takes time but then most things that are worth it do, don't they? Sir Ken Robinson, the education consultant on the arts, widely known for his perfect speeches at the popular TED conferences, once spoke about when television was launched in America. According to Sir Ken, those in the radio industry warned that this new television invention would never catch on. Their reasoning was that the good, hardworking people of America were simply too busy to sit around all day watching television. At least with radio they could listen and do at the same time. Only, they did find time of course. Lots of time. On average just over five hours every day now in fact. There are still the same twenty four hours in the day but they carved out the time to just sit and watch. Presumably certain things stopped being done or were put off. However, every day we are faced with this challenge of doing something or putting it off. It would appear to be a simple enough, harmless choice to make, the choice, however, is only the first part of the process. The consequences; the repercussions of making that choice are worth much more consideration than we tend to offer.

Actors would say that this method used to change their current focus or mindset was very similar to the technique of method acting, where they consume themselves in the characteristic of the part they are playing, to help them to deliver as convincing a performance as possible. And there have been a number of problems with this method, which have been publicised over the years: actors developing alcohol or addiction problems, which mimic that of their characters' and developing neurotic tendencies or depression, having played parts with those traits. The ancient Buddhist philosophy of "what we think, we become" is both poignant and literal, however, all too often these warnings and teachings from history end up on a fridge magnet or tattoo, only to become a superficial quotation, collected but not employed. The literally life-changing power of conscious thinking is fascinating and awe-inspiring and plays a key role in being extraordinary.

Now before you start to feel uncomfortable, I'm not going to ask you to challenge your religious or spiritual beliefs and I'm not going to introduce something that will seem so shallow and fluffy that you'll get embarrassed about reading this book and feel that you have to mask the front cover for fear of ridiculing. You will note this book did not come with an accompanying dream catcher or coloured gemstone. What I am about to sketch out for you is a fantastically underused method of changing the way that you think about anything you apply it to. Perhaps most importantly, it is scientific and more than a little inspiring.

Magic

Occasionally you meet people who you can't help but be in awe of and be inspired by. I consider myself extremely fortunate to call Richard McDougall my friend because he's one of those people who is a true defender of meaningful life. You may not have heard of him before, but Richard is a bit of an unsung hero in the world of magic; a former World Open Champion for his exceptionally skilful close-up magic, a Gold Star member of the Inner Magic Circle (the highest level of membership of the world famous 'The Magic Circle') and with television and live performance credits that keep him up there with the very best in the business. Richard is an example of how television is absolutely not a gauge of talent or success, for if it was, Richard would have his own prime-time television show. In fact, I wish he did; I'd much rather watch Richard perform any day than another house price being doubled by fitting bi-folding doors, or a chef traipsing around Italy cooking yet more meals.

Richard is a magician, fellow speaker on body language and director but he also has one of the most intelligently creative minds of anyone I have ever met. In his spare time he is one of the magicians in the Breathe Magic project, established by David Owen a QC and keen magician, originally in response to his interest in the notion of how it might be possible to use magic as therapy, rather than just as an entertainment form. It's a concept, which isn't new, yet remarkably few people know anything about. American illusionist David Copperfield, famous for making the Statue of Liberty disappear (and bringing it back, much to the relief of his legal team, no doubt) formed his very own Project Magic in 1981 to use magic as a form of therapy for people with physical, social and psychological disabilities. The benefits of which were the very same that David Owen wanted to replicate, but here, in England. Armed with a vision, he approached Guy's and St Thomas' NHS Foundation Trust, which has two internationally renowned teaching hospitals in London. Owen specifically felt that magic, as a tool for therapy, might appeal most to children and found himself talking to the lead paediatric occupational therapist at the Evelina Children's Hospital at St Thomas'. The therapist happened to have a keen interest in hemiplegia; a condition that affects one side of the body caused by injury to parts of the brain that control movements of the limbs, trunk, and face etc. Hemiplegia can develop before, during or soon after birth or indeed later in childhood as a result of another injury or illness. It's actually a relatively common condition with approximately 80% of cases being congenital and 20% acquired. The causes of congenital hemiplegia are actually unknown and the first time parents become aware of it, is normally during infancy when their child has difficulty moving one side of their body, which gradually becomes more and more obvious. Acquired hemiplegia can be brought on by brain tumour, childhood stroke or traumatic brain injury, for example. It's often a tragic final blow to an already difficult and upsetting journey. The presentation obviously varies from child to child, depending on the site and extent of the damage to the brain, however, inevitably there is a degree of weakness, stiffness and lack of control on the affected side of the body; children who Richard has worked with in the Breathe Magic project find it difficult to use their affected hand and arm and to use both hands together and as such, are often shy and embarrassed by their inability to carry out simple two-handed tasks that other children can do.

Traditional occupational therapy can be repetitive by its very nature and requires repetitive practice in order to make improvements, which is often difficult for children to remain motivated to do; typically they are initially motivated but quickly lose interest in the exercises. Magic, however, is therapy by stealth; self-reinforcing, intriguing and presented by default as fun, captivating and of course - magical. *Peter, one seven year old boy who Richard taught through the project, had never seen the palm of his hand; the hemiplegia having weakened his hand muscles in such a way that his fingers were permanently firmly closed across his palm. The process of learning how to perform the magic tricks meant that *Peter had to find a way to hold and manipulate objects in order for him to demonstrate the miracles, and his desire to do this was so strong that the occupational therapists used the magic trick itself as the motivator for him to work on and develop his muscles so that he could open his hand. When *Peter's parents came to take him home at the end of the day, the therapists and magicians showed his Mother what *Peter was practicing and why, in order to encourage him to continue practicing the magic trick at home. *Peter's determination to learn the magic trick resulted in him being able to move his fingers away from his palm sufficiently to hold objects in his hand and strengthen his overall hand muscles. The impact this has had, extends way beyond being able to perform a simple magic trick, as *Peter and his Mum have experienced. The team at Breathe Magic have seen results like this several times now including one eight year old girl, Emily*, diagnosed with complex regional pain syndrome. Until one day when Emily* banged her elbow, she led a perfectly able life, free of any disability and she especially enjoyed writing, playing the violin and street dance. Banging her elbow hurt and did cause minor injury but after the injury healed, Emily's* brain was still sending messages that she was in pain. The pain messages continued and worsened until she was unable to physically touch her arm; she could not let anyone near it, or have anything touch it including water or even clothing, without it causing her excruciating pain. Even using a lift would result in screaming agony because of the vibrations caused by the lifts' mechanism. However, it was worse than that for Emily*: simply thinking about her elbow or even moving her hand just a tiny amount caused her pain and distress so intense that her agony caused her to cry. She stopped playing violin and could no longer write. Teachers accused her of acting up and she became withdrawn. Until one day at the Breathe Magic project when one of the occupational therapists at the Evelina ward showed Emily* a magic trick, which involved reaching behind her back. However, once she'd seen the magic trick, she wanted to learn it - and understandably so. What she was saw this: The magician showed her an opaque cardboard box with a lid. Inside the box was a cube and on each face of the cube a different picture. With the magician's back turned, she was asked to think of one of the pictures on the cube, place the cube back into the box and replace the lid, placing the box into the awaiting hands of the magician, held out behind his back. The magician turned around and told Emily* which picture she had chosen. She wanted to learn the trick so much but the occupational therapists knew that it would be a jump too far, so they started by teaching Emily* how to perform smaller magic tricks, which required smaller physical actions in order to gradually build up fractional opening of the fingers on her affected arm. After a few weeks of performing magic tricks, which had been focusing Emily's* mind on other things whilst simultaneously building up muscle function and an increased range of movement, she performed that magic trick that had first impressed her so much, putting the arm that once caused her so much agony, usually held close to her body and largely disabled, behind her back in order to receive the box. Her pain had stopped. The pain messages being sent by her brain had been reset and within days she was back to writing and playing the violin. One little magic trick changed one little girl's entire life. Extraordinary.

The Breathe Magic intensive therapy programme for children with hemiplegia is a ten day camp and comprises the tuition of magic tricks and other bimanual activities (for example, children prepare their own lunch, cut food, carry their own tray, hold a knife and fork etc) and playing games, which requires two hands. The children are also encouraged to make costumes for the performance at the end of the project to staff, patients and their parents. The focus for those participating is not on therapy or on their disability but on what they can achieve and what they want to achieve. For the full ten days, magicians and occupational therapists work one-on-one with the children, teaching them to activate and use the affected side of their body through play and using the children's desire to want to learn the secret to and how to perform magic tricks. Extraordinarily, this revolutionary project produces more substantial and sustained improvements in the children's function than traditional therapy methodologies but there have also been other extraordinary results that no one expected.

As a result of the project, one little boy was moved up an entire reading class in school because his mindset had changed; he now realised that anything was possible and that his life so far had been focused on what he couldn't do and what was not possible, rather than what was possible. The psychosocial impact of therapies like this and thinking differently is huge. My friend Richard points out that there is an interesting paradox in that magic is all about doing the impossible and here they are running a project which shows children how to give themselves permission to do just that. I ask Richard what is extraordinary about the project for him: "Pride is a great sensation: to see pride in others who have achieved something is really uplifting and that gives pride to me." What a gift. The future is exciting for Breathe Magic, with a project for adults who have had strokes currently being developed and a separate project, which will see the team working with children with mental health issues. In a trial project they saw extraordinary results, which were hugely encouraging: children arrived, some wearing sunglasses, a few sat in wheelchairs and others not moving, motionless in their seats. There was little to no interaction between the children but magic has changed their lives. Within three sessions the children were out of their wheelchairs, had removed their sunglasses and were interacting with each other and the therapists and magicians. Would that and the other changes to these children's lives have happened without the magic project? Possibly but however positive I am, I feel it would have been highly unlikely. Seeing children discover their capabilities and seeing the impact that has on their own lives and that of their parents must be fantastically rewarding - for all involved. A magician for over twenty years, Richard has realised that magic is not about fooling your audience's brain - but more about fooling your own brain. It's all about looking at it from a different point of view.

*To protect their identities I have used fictional names for the children involved.

Humility

Florence Foster Jenkins always longed to be an opera singer. She received music lessons as a child and dreamed of studying opera abroad. However, growing up in the late eighteen hundreds, her Father, Charles Foster, a wealthy businessman, forbid her a career in the entertainment industry, so she eloped to Philadelphia with a physician named Frank Thornton Jenkins. Florence went on to marry Frank, however, the marriage only lasted seven years. I don't know for sure but I suspect her singing may have had something to do with it. You see, Florence was not technically brilliant. In fact, listening to some of her recordings even from later in her career, she was awful. So awful that the fame she gathered was in fact due to her lack of rhythm, pitch and tone, becoming famous for the amusement she provided, rather than any skill. Imagine living with that for seven years.

In 1909 her Father died and Florence inherited a significant sum of money; sufficient to pay for her to take voice lessons, ironically, and involve herself with the musical circles of New York in the early nineteen hundreds. When her Mother passed away in 1928, Florence inherited the remainder of the family fortune, which helped to boost her singing career; despite her lack of skill, that is exactly what she carved. She began to sell performances in hotels and small music halls, gathering a large fan base who came to witness the woman who performed so sincerely as a professional opera singer, ridiculing her for her inability to actually sing. However, in 1944, at the age of seventy six, Florence performed to a sold out audience at the world famous Carnegie Hall, where apparently, some two thousand fans who had not booked tickets were turned away at the door. Widely regarded as one of the worst singers in the world (the author Steven Pile went a confident step further declaring her as "the world's worst opera singer"), her fan base was quite ironic, with press reviews ranging from: "Her singing was hopelessly lacking in semblance of pitch" to "No one, before or since, has succeeded in liberating themselves quite so completely from the shackles of musical notation." Despite or because of this, the self-styled Madame Jenkins became a byword for artistic ambition and self-delusion, yet she always considered herself a star, which, in an unusual twist of reality, is just what she became. Her pursuit of her childhood dream, despite being unable to fulfil it on a technical level, was what made Florence so extraordinary. Of her Carnegie Hall performance, which was to be her last, the New York World Telegram wrote: "She was exceedingly happy in her work. It is a pity so few artists are. And her happiness was communicated as if by magic to her listeners… who were stimulated to the point of audible cheering, even joyous laughter and ecstasy by the inimitable singing."

Florence Foster Jenkins died one month after her sell out performance at Carnegie Hall. She had prearranged an epitaph, which read: "Some may say I couldn't sing, but no one can say that I didn't sing." The only person who gives us permission to be extraordinary; to pursue something more and break from the constraints of ordinary - or not to - is us.

We Dare To Try

When you first meet Robert Williams, you wonder if he's an assistant or a roadie to a rock band. He looks ordinary; the sort of person you'd pass on the street and completely forget about if asked to retrace your steps. I realise that sounds almost - well, offensive, however, you just can't help expect the founder of The Kindness Offensive to look nothing short of extraordinary. It does just go to show how appearances can be so deceptive.

I met Robert when he created what can only be described as a completely unexpected, emotionally engaging, soul-shaking spectacle at TEDxMiltonKeynes, where his colleague, David Goodfellow spoke after me. As David described to the audience what The Kindness Offensive did, Robert sounded an airhorn. Indoors. It was loud. Very loud. And into the auditorium piled some fifty or more people sporting smiles, hard hats, fluorescent yellow waistcoats and blowing party whistles. That was pretty surprising but it had nothing on what they were doing: they were handing out shiny, wrapped packages as fast as their hands would allow. People in the audience were tearing open these free gifts and finding kettles, blenders, vacuum cleaners; even a television! Brand new, unopened and absolutely free. We had to do nothing for them; simply sit back and enjoy being thoroughly spoilt. And then, as David attempted to continue telling an audience full of giggling, over-excited adults who had been instantly transported back to a Christmas when they were five or six, explosions of confetti and glitter rained across the audience. As a behaviourist, I couldn't help but sit and watch in complete amazement - and admittedly, puzzlement - at the reaction this team of people were eliciting from us. It was a truly magical experience and the constant reiteration from David that these gifts were free and ours to keep and that they didn't want anything in return, forced a lot of soul searching for a lot of people. This is the epitome of true kindness.

However, it wasn't a one-off finale. This is what Robert and his team do all year round. They are responsible for having given away almost six million pounds worth of items to date and for making a lot of people, all over the world, very happy indeed. They're featured in national newspapers, with full page spreads in The Sun, the Indian Times, the Big Issue and the Independent and featured on the BBC, ITN, FOX and in many more international media outlets. None of the six thousand strong worldwide team are paid, giving up their time freely to spread the message of kindness and happiness. But why? And how on earth do they manage to get all of these products? It's not sponsorship; it's not by association and it's not endorsement. So how do you go about getting free televisions, buildings (yes, buildings) or top of the range running machines and why would you give them away?

Robert is one of the most genuine, peaceful people I have had the pleasure of meeting. He's calm, honest and with a strikingly straight forward and sincere approach to his outlook on life. He tells me that it all started a few years ago when he was struggling to make ends meet. As a freelance writer and musician, it was a series of unfortunate, yet expensive, events that led him to discover that you can get things for free, if only you ask. He didn't have the money to get a particular piece of hardware he required to fix his broken computer and then found himself way off from the amount needed to replace his car's broken carburettor. And then there was the time he was hungry, had nothing to eat and no money to get food in. What did Robert do? Did he panic? Did he steal? Did he plunge into a world of desperation? "I called people and told them the truth - I didn't want to lie to them and while some people didn't want to help me, after a few telephone calls I soon discovered people who were confused by what I was saying. They were surprised that I was so candid and just asking for their help. So they helped me and sent me what I needed, for free."

Robert soon ended up with a surplus of things that he gave to friends, including David Goodfellow, who became especially interested in the notion that receiving free things and then giving them away brought happiness to them and to the recipients. David pondered, over free pizza, whether this process could become a thing to do, for other people. A job, of sorts. Could Robert and David become the real life, modern day version of Robin Hood? It's a humble idea and seems worlds apart from bankers and their big bonuses and corrupt board members and politicians fiddling expenses.

When I pushed David on why it was that they gave it any serious thought and what personal journey or analysis he had gone on in order to arrive at the decision to dedicate so much time, effort and resources to this, his reply was enlightening: "Being nice and kind and altruistic are all good things to do, so naturally Robert and I were keen to do anything like that but it raised further questions, which were interesting to consider, such as: Is being kind a good idea? Or is it just something that sounds good? We wanted to challenge those questions and set ourselves some targets that tested the argument but at the same fulfilled the purpose: Can we get enough food to fill the soup kitchen? Can we get a company to give us enough toys to enable us to give one to every child in the local hospital? So initially those things were good for us but good for other people at the same time." And so this notion of receiving goods and then giving them away became very much a twofold process; firstly to decide on a project that would make them feel good and would benefit others and then to test it to see if it is indeed possible. As Robert quite rightly states: "We start with absolutely nothing and the result, the impact, is huge." I put it to Robert that what they were doing was extraordinary on so many levels but his typically casual response was straight forward and simple: "We dare to try; that's all. Where other people think things can't be done or will be too much effort, they give up - they don't even try." It would be easy to mistakenly think that The Kindness Offensive are on a moral crusade to change or challenge our way of thinking but David disagrees: "We're not in the business of changing anyone's mind. If you make enough calls, you'll find someone with a similar moral compass to yourself and they will be willing to help you out - sometimes we'll set out to get something and if the mood is that this is going to be tough and might take some time, that invariably is the result: it takes longer than expected to achieve and we all find it hard work. Conversely, if we need to see urgent results or we want to get some things urgently, we'll end up getting them much sooner." If that's not a perfect, socially beneficial example of the effect of determination and focus, I don't know what is. Their greatest successes tend to happen when the team of volunteers work as a group because when there are multiple telephone whisperers, the title given to the volunteers on the telephones doing the calling to suppliers, the group dynamic changes. It seems to create a sense of camaraderie and a reminder of the common goal, which motivates everyone to continue.

Interestingly and surprisingly, it's not all been plain sailing for The Kindness Offensive. They have discovered that some members of society and groups push back, resisting their great work. Likely through cynicism that something couldn't ever really be that good without an evil agenda. David shares with me some of the criticisms they've had, which range from "you're not a charity" and "you're not a formal organisation," to "you're commercialising the concept of kindness and encouraging children to want at Christmas" and my personal favourite: "you're not a vegan." Vegans can be especially weird. The team have also experienced plenty of people offering advice on what they should do and how they should do it but as Robert shrewdly points out: "the majority of people telling us what we should do and how to do it, when asked, hadn't actually exceeded at anything themselves. We had done so much compared to their so little and largely because we do it - we don't just think about it or talk about it; we dare to try it."

The impact that The Kindness Offensive and their extraordinary way of thinking has had is extreme and goes much further than handing out free gifts to people. Their regular gift giving ceremonies to children's wards, charities and organisations mean that they could quite literally make or break christmas for thousands and it's not an exaggeration to say that some wouldn't be alive today, having perished from starvation, of the cold or without having the luxury of a plan B. That's an extremely important, poignant and heavy responsibility that lays at their door. It's one thing getting free pizza delivered, or being able to fix your car because of the generosity of a local mechanic. But becoming responsible for others' is a whole different moral game. The impact it has had on those volunteering for The Kindness Offensive has been just as deep, however. I ask David how it has changed him and he pauses to reflect. "It made me ask myself how free am I? What possibilities exist to me personally? It has totally changed my mindset and I'm a different person as a result of thinking differently. For example, I feel freedom in creativity and thinking and in being able to do whatever I want to do by just darling to do things. I'm welcome in more board rooms than I ever was before, girls like me more and I'm in a better place emotionally and psychologically, with more socially important knowledge than I had before." Robert, unsurprisingly if you ever meet him, says: "I've been thinking this way for as long as I can remember. I absolutely expected this to happen and while I'm fascinated by it, I'm not at all surprised because the reason a lot of things don't happen is because people don't bother to make them happen. There's actually a lot of kindness in the world."

What these two men started and have continued to encourage, is extraordinary. But what next? David's answer is ambitious as much as it is ordinary for them: "everything." Their drive is to give everyone in the world free presents and to encourage governments and organisations to consider making happiness and kindness part of the curriculum. Robert especially wants to see ambassadors for kindness, to encourage others to do the same. In the meantime, it's business as usual; they'll keep doing what they do because there's still so much opportunity to do it. David is keen to further push the boundaries. He's especially interested in finding out if this process has a glass ceiling because: "as big as we've dared to dream, we've realised each of those dreams." What do you think they should do next? How could you help this cause? I know Robert and David would love to hear from you to find out what ideas you have about how to further spread a life-changing message that really does make you stop and think. Kettles, blenders, televisions, games consoles; even a building with all of the bills paid for! While it's a leap in physicality, it is simply an extension of the same thing, which just goes to show how limitless realisation is when matched with ambition.

In December 2014, The Kindness Offensive will be conducting the largest toy give away plant earth has ever seen.

Service, Please

Danny Meyer is little known here in England, unless of course you're in the hospitality industry, for Danny is somewhat of a legend to restauranteurs all over the world. He's written an internationally best-selling book and is the founder of some of the hottest, award-winning names in the restaurant world, including New York's Union Square Cafe, Gramercy Tavern, Eleven Madison Park, Tabla and The Modern. However, it's not clear success for running restaurants that makes his story so extraordinary. If there's one thing that is common among ordinary people, it is that they give up quickly. When faced with an obstacle, they see that as permanent. Often dispirited and dejected, they stop on their journey and continue as they were before. I've lost count of the thousands of people I've spoken to in the last few years who have told me of how their dreams didn't go to plan, or how their desire to do something was quashed and became "impossible." Impossible? I say improbable. With time and money, I think we'd all struggle to find many things that were impossible. We don't even know if time travel is impossible because it hasn't yet been proven otherwise. Look at Cher - people thought her coming out of retirement (the first time around) was impossible. Fortunately they didn't have long to wait. That's a key characteristic among ordinary people; they give up too easily.

Danny Meyer had an idea for a restaurant, which he thought was really good. It was 1985 and he was just twenty seven years old. So far it's a pretty unremarkable story setting; I had some pretty big ideas when I was twenty seven - in fact you probably did, too! The young people I meet when I work with youth groups or young offenders, mostly all have ideas of world peace, being a millionaire, or becoming a pop star. Just like most people that age, Danny had next to no experience of running a restaurant and had absolutely no experience of opening one. Yet that's exactly what he did. Union Square Cafe would become one of New York City's most revered restaurants. While there's no doubt that his upbringing helped shape his interests and direction, with a father in the hotel industry and regularly eating out, Danny's is not a fairytale rags to riches story of plain sailing. In his excellent book Setting the Table, Danny reflects on that exact moment when he decided to quit his $125,000 a year job and stop applying to law school: "It would be nearly two years before I would have a location, a name, or a menu for my restaurant, but instinctively I knew how I would run the business. It would reflect the confluence of interests, passion, pleasure and family dynamics that had shaped my life." This is part of what makes all ordinary people achieve extraordinary things. They aren't from a special planet, fed enhancing drugs, or trained by a special "Be Extraordinary" school; they act from what they know is intrinsically true to them. They act from the heart. And while they may not always get it right, as Danny's own story shows, they persevere, perhaps learning and adapting as they go. Ultimately, being extraordinary, in whatever endeavour and whoever you choose, is about being true to you. How many of us, at twenty seven, in 1985, faced with a $700,000 bill just for the lease, design and construction of a restaurant, would have continued with this "good idea?" I had a great idea once that involved the only open window in my parent's house, a tower of garden furniture and an additional bunk-up by a friend, followed by a small leap from the garden chair, balanced at the top of the tower. I'm not sure I'd trust myself with $700,000 and a good idea. In fact, some of my ideas are so far out there, that all projects have to be run past my assistant first. Steph is my grounding plate and sensible sounding board and without her, I'm almost certain I'd be in hospital through exhaustion and probably bankrupt to boot.

For someone who is now known the world over as one of the leading authority figures in hospitality, Danny has plenty of stories of poor customer service, misguided management and problems from his history, including this little chestnut, which I just have to share with you: "One evening, some weeks after we opened, I was proudly showing off Union Square Cafe to Tom Carouso, a good friend from Trinity College who had just returned to New York after living in Africa, who couldn't believe I had actually followed through on my dream of opening a restaurant. The two of us were surveying the restaurant from the balcony overlooking the back dining room with its twenty five foot ceiling and its huge mural along the back wall. As I began to describe how the artist Judy Rifka had painted it, I suddenly heard a piercing crack, and a boom, as one end of a thirty foot track lighting rod ripped out of the ceiling and swung down like a pendulum. The heavy steel rod and its fixtures smashed into the wall with a grotesque thud, gouging a three inch gash in the plaster wall, perilously close to the head of a woman who was dining. If it had been two inches to the right it could well have killed her…" Never before has my maxim of putting things into context been more relevant: Did anyone die?

I've intentionally chosen not to include examples of how ordinary people can do extraordinarily bad things. I made a conscious decision while researching for this book to focus on the positives because I believe that many who read this will be inspired to fulfil their own desires, which may well be completely different from whatever it is that they do now. Some may change their perspective, alter their way of working or set out to improve their personal or home lives. This is what I hope will happen. However, I recognise that the common definition of extraordinary is something which is "very unusual or remarkable" and while that encompasses things that are "amazing," "marvellous," "wonderful" and "miraculous," it also covers more subjective synonyms such as: "unbelievable," "astonishing," "astounding" and "exceptional." These could well be used to describe something good or indeed bad. While our time here is finite, why would you choose to focus on the negative things?

In Mind

When we put our minds to it, it really is quite remarkable what we can achieve. Take weight loss as an example. Dieting and weight loss are global fascinations. According to a poll by Mintel, in the UK alone it is estimated that one in four adults are actively dieting at any one time. The poll showed that up to thirteen million people are on a permanent diet and according to consumer market research group NPD, approximately 22% of the population of the United States of America are actively dieting at any one time. If you pardon the pun, it is a big business and like most of the things we wish to gain control of or change, we reach out for assistance or for someone to do the hard work for us. I suppose this is why diet pills, books, regimes, weight loss DVDs, clubs and other paraphernalia that preys on the hopeful, are so lucrative. We want the easy route. However, when it comes to weight loss, in much the same way as combatting addiction, the real work happens inside your mind - not your body. Let me explain...

If you think you need to go on a diet we will assume that you are overweight, which, without wanting to cast huge assertions, is probably quite accurate otherwise you wouldn't want to lose weight. Unless you are one of the growing number of painfully slim and attractive people who eat like a sparrow yet still consider themselves to be fat because when they leant over to pick up a piece of lettuce off of the floor, for "lunch," caught glimpse of a reflection of themselves and saw two pieces of skin fold. As a result of that, you think, to varying degrees, that you are fat. In turn, because you think you are fat, you are most probably unhappy with the way that you look. That's not an especially positive way of thinking. This negative mindset is not momentary: whenever you look at yourself in the mirror; bathe or get dressed, you see yourself in a less than ideal way. It reinforces that feeling of not being happy with how you look. In turn, you feel despondent and lacking in self confidence about things surrounding your weight: your appearance, your weight and the clothes you wear. You begin eating foods which are comforting and high in fats, sugars and carbohydrates, which don't help with your weight loss. You begin to go out less because of your lack of self-confidence about the way that you look. A lack of exercise and eating comforting foods, exacerbate your weight problem and the vicious cycle continues. You become more and more unhappy because the weight loss you so desire doesn't happen. As a result your mood changes and you become sad, which, in turn, plunges your self-esteem into a downwards spiral and you start taking less care of your appearance. Now all of that begins in your mind. Compare this with a positive outlook. You set yourself a weight and date goal; to be a certain weight by a specific date. You write it down and spend some time visualising the way you want to look, reflecting on how looking that way will make you feel and spend some time reflecting in turn on those feelings of satisfaction and happiness. You read your goal several times each and every day. You allow yourself one day of failure each week to make your goals more realistic; after all, no one is perfect. You focus on every good thing that you eat, rather than the things you should not eat and each day you see as a milestone on your journey towards a fitter, healthier and happier self. If you imagine a spiral as a visual metaphor for both examples; one is distinctly an upwards spiral and the other a downwards one.

This goal setting strategy isn't restricted to losing weight, however. You can apply it to anything you want to achieve, or set out to do, or to get other people to do. This technique of setting a very specific goal, with a deadline and supporting yourself on the journey to your determined goal, is very often central to making that step change from ordinary to extraordinary because that is in itself a journey of sorts. You will need to change the way that you think about and respond to obstacles, opportunities and the way in which you apply your knowledge and experience. Think of all of the things you could have achieved; the places you could have visited and the things you could have done if you had set yourself really clear, measurable goals in this way. The applications are wide-ranging and apply to teachers, leadership teams, students, business owners and every individual who has aspirations or dreams. I dare say that includes you - I'd like to think it does.

Think Big

Paul Potts won the hit talent television show, Britain's Got Talent, in 2007, with his beautiful performance of Nessun dorma, an aria from Puccini's opera Turandot. Thanks to my good friend Rachel, I am quite a fan of Puccini's works and like millions of other viewers, was blown away by the unexpected power of Paul's voice. His personal story is so inspiring that it was translated into a motion picture for cinema release; One Chance. However, Paul's story is just one example of those who try for many years before becoming "an overnight success." Passionate about becoming a professional singer, Paul publicly revealed that he spent most of his life-savings on singing lessons including an understandably expensive master class with one of the finest opera singers this world has ever seen, the legendary Luciano Pavarotti. Shy and an unlikely looking star, Paul Potts pursued his dream of singing and encouraged by friends and family while recovering from a broken collar bone following an accident, applied to take part in Britain's Got Talent. Had he not made that decision, he may well still be the manager of his local Carphone Warehouse store, where he worked prior to his big break. The result for Paul is what certainly appears to be a move from an ordinary life to a quite extraordinary one, with two number one albums to his name.

Paul Potts is an ordinary person, just like you and I. However, so too are the likes of Richard Branson, Walt Disney, Thomas Edison and Donald Trump. It is simply that they approach things in quite a different way. Donald Trump once answered a question about how he had become so successful with this strikingly inquisitive answer: "most people think small, because most people are afraid of success, afraid of making decisions, afraid of winning... that gives people like me a great advantage." The reason it gives Donald a great advantage is because, by his own admission, he "thinks big." Sometimes in order to get extraordinary results we need to think big.

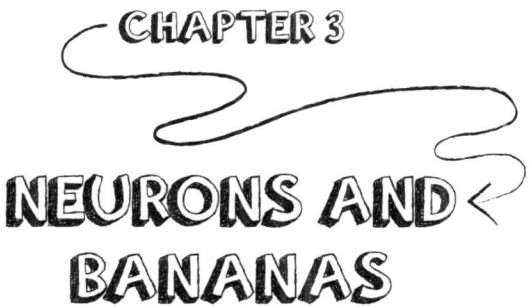

CHAPTER 3

NEURONS AND BANANAS

"The most wonderful thing in the world is somebody who knows who they are and knows what they were created to do."

Bishop T. D. Jakes.

Intelligence

I was invited to speak at a TEDx conference recently. If you have lived your life without coming across TED, which stands for Technology, Entertainment, Design, I can promise you that your life is about to get a whole lot richer. The organisers believe that those three broach subject areas (technology, entertainment and design) are, collectively, shaping our future. Under the slogan of "ideas worth spreading," TED conferences are held twice a year in different countries around the world. The conferences bring together some of the most innovative, curious and interesting thinkers and doers, to present their ideas. The events have been described as "the ultimate brain spa" and "a journey into the future, in the company of those creating it." TEDx are independently organised, local versions of the global TED conferences; that is what the little x denotes.

I spoke first, which was useful for a number of reasons, not least because I knew that I wasn't in danger of repeating anyone else's points but mainly because it allowed me to relax and enjoy the rest of the day as a member of the audience. During one of the scheduled refreshment breaks, I got talking to one of the guests about intelligence. She raised a point which I thought was quite interesting; she said: "despite the wide mix of intelligence in this room, we are essentially all the same." Now, as one of the speakers, I considered how best to reply to this, rather inaccurate statement so that it didn't appear that I was being overly defensive, or indeed trying to appear righteous in some way. What I said was this: "well, apart from the wide mix of intelligence, which, actually means we are all quite different." I understood her point; she was referring to the group of speakers and guests as a collective sample of the human species and by "we are essentially all the same" she was narrowing the often incurred intelligence rift where people assume a higher authority because of an increased intelligence. The attitude of 'I am intelligent therefore I am better than you' probably should be one of my pet hates alongside hose pipes and wire coat hangers, just to add insult to injury. It is attributed to many people but somewhere, someone, once said that credentials on a wall do not necessarily make you a decent human being. And from my experience they certainly do not guarantee you will be any good at your job either. However, her statement, all-be-it well intended, was fundamentally flawed. It is okay that the group were all very different and in fact, I embraced that, seeing an opportunity to meet a wide variety of people with an even wider variety of backgrounds, experience and intelligence. However, the group of speakers were not only different to each other and the guests, who were in turn different to the speakers and had their own pockets of specialist knowledge, but they were different in a physical way, too.

Seeking ways to be extraordinary stimulates us in arguably the same way that learning does, simply because it is in itself a process of seeking out new knowledge and provides opportunity for reflective thinking. In turn this can also enrich our environments and both of those things lead the brain to grow. And not just in one area. The American research psychologist Mark Rosenzweig demonstrated through experiments with rats that stimulating the brain makes it grow in nearly every conceivable way. Acetycholine is a brain chemical essential for learning; it is like the diesel of learning and it is higher in rats trained on difficult spatial problems than in rats trained on problems that are much simpler. Rosenzweig discovered that animals that are raised in enriched environments with swings, ladders, objects to explore and companionship, learn better than genetically identical animals in environments without active enrichment. As Dr. Norman Doidge writes in his outstanding book *The Brain That Changes Itself*: "Mental training or life in enriched environments increases brain weight by five percent in the cerebral cortex of animals and up to nine percent in areas that the training directly stimulates." The reason this brain weight happens is because of an increased blood flow to certain areas of the brain. Just how a bucket gets heavier the more water you put in. The increased blood flow is there to support the twenty five percent more branches and size increase of the trained or stimulated neurons of those areas of the brain affected by the stimulation or enrichment. Doidge also reveals that postmortem examinations have shown that education "increases the number of branches among neurons." This is significant because an increased number of branches drives those neurons further apart, which in turn leads to an increase in the volume and density of the brain. While you are most unlikely to have an increased brain size at the top of your goals list when it comes to reasons to be extraordinary, it does help prove my point and qualify that there is method in my madness to the years of research into understanding what extraordinary is.

So you see, in many cases we can be very different indeed. The more your brain is enriched and stimulated, the heavier it becomes or in brain terms, the 'bigger' it becomes. However, a larger brain does not make you a better person and nor does it automatically assume you rights. I have met many a fantastically intelligent person who turned out to be a complete and utter arse.

Be Amazed

Our brains characterise us. A healthy body and conscious intent are all but useless if we do not have the control or purpose of our brains. It is a truly extraordinary thing, the brain. It only weights three pounds. That's less than a quarter of a stone. Just over one kilogram. If you have never seen a brain - and if you have I hope it was a photograph - it looks a little bit like a walnut. Out of its shell. It feels, however, quite like blancmange. It has a slightly squishy give to it and very smooth surface. I once heard a parent telling their child that the brain was a muscle. It isn't and whenever my mind wanders, I often think of that child and what they ended up doing. They were probably snapped up as a senior decision maker within the NHS. The brain is in fact a massive collection of cells called neurons. Your brain and mine are probably quite similar looking and are made up of a similar number of, wait for it, one hundred billion neurons. One hundred billion things that make you work; that form your beliefs, passions, knowledge, opinions, ability to learn and your behaviour, all contained behind your face. One hundred billion neurons. That's fifteen times the total number of people on earth. Now that is extraordinary.

It gets even more incredible though. Each of those cells makes contact with ten thousand or so other brain cells via a specialised system of communication connections called synapses. There are about sixty thousand miles worth of fibres, which make up the components which form our brains. All of that goes around with you everywhere you go. It continues working under water, upside down and while being spun around three hundred and sixty five days a year; our brains are undeniably the most comprehensive, intelligent and highly portable computer known to man. So why on earth settle for ordinary when you have something quite so incredible at your disposal?

A Man in Uniform

We listen to people that stand out. We listen to people who are loud and command attention and we listen to people in roles of authority. Psychologist Leonard Bickman tested the power of authority on us in perhaps one of the most well-known social psychology experiments; you may have heard of it. He had one of his research assistants stand in the street and ask passers by to do things, such as pick up a piece of rubbish, give some money to a stranger or move away from a bus stop. The research assistant repeated the same experiments over and over but wore either civilian clothes, a milkman's uniform or the uniform of a guard. The results of the experiment were clear: 19% obeyed the assistant when he was dressed in his civilian clothes; 14% obeyed him dressed as a milkman and 38% obeyed him when he was dressed as a guard.

While the results may not be overly surprising - after all, any decent, civilised person has been raised to respect those in authority - there are several other research studies which support this notion that our behaviour and opinions are influenced by how others are dressed. In their enlightening study, Leff, Nydegger and Buck (1970) found that people perceived nurses to be less caring when dressed casually. Perhaps somewhat ironically, Stillman and Resnick (1972) found that there was actually no difference in the willingness of people to disclose information to counsellors based on how they were dressed. When I say no matter how they were dressed, naturally I mean whether they were casually dressed or wearing something more professional. Clearly no-one would feel comfortable readily sharing personal information with a counsellor who was dressed as a squirrel, or Elvis.

This research into how what we wear affects the behaviour of others is likely to have prompted, or at least encouraged, further research into the psychology of colour. It is a vast field, which is concerned with how colour impacts mood, feeling and behaviour. I have to admit to being a little skeptical. Like many elements of accessible science, it does appear to have been adopted so widely and some of the research used so prescriptively, that the whole subject now seems a little unchecked and of course highly subjective. Similarly, when Neuro Linguistic Programming (NLP) became popular, you don't have to look too far to find someone who will gladly take your money to tell you that blue means you are sad, purple means you are creative and green is, well, for grass. Despite my slightly flippant view on it, mainly because the snake oil hacks repel me, there is some genuine scientific research in this area, which is just why you see light green and blue often used in medical facilities and purple in therapy rooms. Humans are wonderfully complex and we are, ironically like everyone else, unique. To this end, one rule simply does not and cannot apply to us all. If you look at one source, it tells you that you should wear blue if you want to communicate new ideas and concepts but that it should only be electric or royal blue. White is reserved for formal presentations. Red is the colour of passion and intensity, so if you have an emotional message to present you should wear something that is red. Pink though, now that is the real secret weapon, apparently. According to one source it is the most effective colour to wear whenever money is the subject; in a sales pitch, for example. Apparently Donald Trump wears a pink tie very often. However, a quick Google search would suggest that he doesn't wear pink all that more often than some other colours and if the images are anything to go by, he actually wears red most often. Of course, he might just like the colour pink - or red. Did anyone think of that?

One source even unhelpfully suggests that "too much of the colour red can cause us to become irritated, agitated and ultimately angry. Too little and we become cautious, manipulative and fearful." It negates to define what is too much or too little. Despite many promises to empower yourself with the knowledge of colour psychology, it would appear, from a scientific perspective at least, that we should be aware that colour can influence how we feel and our behaviour too, but you would be cautioned to live your life prescriptively wearing certain colours expecting a specific outcome. It is important to recognise that there is undoubtedly something quite relevant in our relationship with colour. I for one would find it difficult to take the instructions of a police officer seriously if their uniform was pink, for example. Have you ever been offered a glass of water, which was cloudy or murky? I remember once having a cup of tea made for me by one of my clients at her home. She had misplaced her glasses and struggled with making the tea, presumably guessing at items and using familiarity to guide her. In the process of removing things from cupboards and moving around the kitchen she had knocked all sorts of things over. My tea finally arrived and we sat talking. I got about half way through my mug of tea and felt something hit my lips. I peered into my cup and all seemed as it should, however, suspicious, I poked around with a shard of a rich tea biscuit. A handful of white, fleshy maggots floated to the surface. I shook with surprise so forcibly that a slosh of tea fell onto her carpet, which is when she enquired what was wrong. She saw the spilt tea quite well enough. On further investigation they were in fact grains of rice that had been knocked into the cup and swollen with the tea. I have never been so relieved, thankful and pleased to see rice in my tea. It is interesting (and evolutionary important), that we perceive brown things to be dirty, white things to be clean (or maggots), red things are hot while yellow and black things are dangerous. Our interpretation of colour is innately still very primitive, however, strongly guides our opinions and behaviours.

Despite what some would like to tell you, there is in fact insufficient evidence that a one on one relationship exists between one particular colour and an emotion. Our responses to colours are ultimately because of our individual culture and our physiological and psychological make-up. It would appear that much of what we know is based on what we have learnt from nature, so trusting your instinct is probably as scientific as you are likely to need to get until more conclusive research is conducted into our relationship with colours.

Inhaling Oxytocin

The neuroscientist Paul Zak is director of the Center for Neuroeconomics Studies at Claremont Graduate University, California. He tells a story about being involved in a pigeon drop con when he as a teenager (which has nothing to do with actual pigeons), while working at a fuel station. A man came out of the toilets holding a pearl necklace, stating he had found it on the floor. Fortuitously the phone rang at that same moment; it was a gentleman enquiring if anyone had found a pearl necklace. He had just brought the necklace as a gift for his wife for their wedding anniversary and was willing to offer a $200 reward for its safe return. Paul Zak, young and eager to do the right thing, was only too happy to help. He informed the person on the telephone that, coincidentally, a gentleman had just found it on the floor in the toilet. "I'll be there in thirty minutes!" came the reply from the other end of the 'phone.

Just when everything seems to be going to plan, the man who had found the necklace said that he was late for a job interview and could not wait for the owner; he had to leave. But what to do with the necklace? "I could give you the necklace to return to its owner and we could split the reward?" suggested the man. Zak thought this was an ingenious idea; he would make $100 and get to bask in the reflected glory of the man who found the necklace. Not having $100 for the man's share of the reward, Zak took the money from the till, as a temporary loan until the reward arrived when he would immediately replace it. He handed the man his half of the reward in exchange for the necklace. The man drove off to his job interview and all was well.

However, the man who had lost the necklace did not in fact show up. Zak called the police, who informed him that the pearl necklace was not real and worth just a few dollars. Naturally embarrassed and deflated, Zak confessed to his employer and agreed to repay the money from his wages. Fast forward some years and today Paul Zak is a leading authority on the neurobiology of trust (and I dare say well educated in the subject in many respects). Somewhat understandably, Zak is interested in discovering why cons like the pigeon drop work and he believes it may be down to the hormone oxytocin. His studies have shown that it is oxytocin which is responsible for making our acts of cooperation feel good; when you feel trusted, your brain releases oxytocin and that in turn causes you to reciprocate the trust. Zak and his colleagues discovered that if you inhale oxytocin, in a laboratory experiment - it is no longer the sixties - your generosity to strangers goes through the roof!

Aside from carrying around a cylinder of oxytocin and an oxygen mask, how can we apply this? Well, Zak and his team have identified that oxytocin is released when you help others and that in turn makes you feel good, so the phrase "I need your help" is an especially potent stimulus. In the case of the pigeon drop con which Zak was lured into, oxytocin was abound in his brain: he was helping the man who found the necklace to reunite it with its owner; he was helping the owner to get his lost wedding anniversary gift back and he would be rewarded in cash for his actions. Perhaps that is why the pigeon drop con doesn't actually involve pigeons: people would be less likely to go out of their way to reunite a pigeon with its owner than a pearl necklace. Such is our drive for material greed. I actually quite like pigeons.

The take home message which can be applied to our journey to be extraordinary is that oxytocin is key to building social relationships with other people; we have an innate predisposition to empathise with others and indeed trust them. While some people do appear to be overly trustworthy, or gullible, it is not their fault; it is as a result of their biological make-up and environmental factors, too.

Fillings and Bed Pans

When I first considered what the difference was between ordinary and extraordinary, I thought about what most people would consider 'normal' people are. What you do obviously helps determine just how ordinary you are, so I started considering the jobs people had. Those with a nine to five state job or a job that is certainly within our scope of expected jobs, which we come into contact with regularly, I felt was a good start for what most would agree was ordinary. I am sure there will be letters but in an attempt to be clear, referring to people as 'ordinary' was only for the purposes of discovering exactly what extraordinary is. I would hate to think that you have an image of me nonchalantly casting my eye over people as they walk past my bay window, with a kaftan casually thrown across one shoulder and my little finger raised as I sip a cup of rare tea and announce in a presumptuous way: "ordinary" or "extraordinary."

When I thought more about the people carrying out these ordinary jobs, I felt they were someone who had no overly unusual hobbies, or who did not have wild ambitions. Their thoughts, beliefs and behaviours should be safe and expected. I did not feel that class was relevant, as there are plenty of examples of people who were raised in impoverished conditions who went on to do very well for themselves; take Charlie Chaplin and Harry Houdini as two examples from history and Bill Cullen, the author of the best-selling book *It's A Long Way From Penny Apples*, as just one of many more recent examples. My definition of ordinary is, hopefully, acceptable to you. I certainly felt it was, well - ordinary. I am using extraordinary then to describe anyone that does something unusual or has a drive or ambition - but with a caveat. By definition someone who is not ordinary could well be extraordinary, however, my definition of extraordinary is more specific; not simply more than ordinary. I am focusing on remarkable jobs or remarkable acts - things that are very unusual, which earn the label of extraordinary. Individuals who go the extra mile or actively go out of their way to buck a trend, or spot a way to do something differently that may, or may not, benefit others. It may be a teacher who knows that by spending their own time filling the classroom with balloons, will ensure her pupils better understand the principles of atoms. Or a husband who actively finds time to reflect, consider his actions and learn to respond better to the actions of his wife.

I feel I can be honest with you, mainly because I don't know you: striving for clarity in the precise definition of just what extraordinary is has been challenging and at times impossible. Take nurses, doctors or indeed any medical staff, for example. While their jobs could be considered ordinary because they are well known and we like to think that we understand them, I would argue that those working in emergency departments, critical care wards and surgical theatres are quite extraordinary. What they do every day, which is normal for them; saving lives, changing lives for the better and prolonging mobility, health and life itself, in the face of budget cuts, staffing cuts and stress is, surely, extraordinary? Conversely, although their role is worthwhile and we should still be grateful for their skill, patience and applied knowledge, a dental nurse, dentist or occupational health nurse are perhaps not as extraordinary, comparatively. They are no less decent a human being but do those roles fall into the category of ordinary? I decided that this was an impossibly subjective route to proceed down and so abandoned trying to categorise people. I felt as though I was playing the role of a work God and when this book was published would be plagued by slashed tyres on my car with just an anonymous dentist's appointment card tucked under my bent and twisted wiper. I did one night wake up with a start, having dreamt that our house was pelted with dirty fillings and bed pans from an angry mob. On reflection, being that specific about what does or does not constitute extraordinary is actually irrelevant. As so much of our own lives is subjective: our achievements, our beliefs and our opinions, it seemed completely unnecessary for me to attempt to define extraordinary that specifically.

As a result, *Be a Purple Banana* is about the principles behind why I think we should all strive to be extraordinary and how you can do so. I am not going to define what extraordinary is, which allows you the freedom of interpretation for yourself but suffice to say it should at the very least fulfil the dictionary definition, which, depending on your favourite dictionary (I hope for your sake that you don't have a favourite dictionary) is something similar to: very unusual or remarkable.

+10%

So what is the difference between those who are ordinary and those who are extraordinary? I believe it is as little as just ten percent.

Many years ago, one drizzly evening in Upminster, in the function room of a social club, I met Barrie Richardson. Barrie is a teacher, university professor and amateur magician. He has been a business and education consultant and manager in industry. He is from and lives in America but on this occasion that I met him, was lecturing in England. A charming, warm hearted man with a spectacular ability to tell stories and clear metaphors, it was Barrie who taught me the +10% Principle. I have lectured on the +10% Principle for nearly ten years and applied it to every area of my own life. Before we get to how to apply it, let me explain what it is and how it works. It offers an explanation of the difference between those in the winner's circle and the also-rans, by defining what the difference is.

The biggest obstacle for most people when aiming to improve something they do or starting something new, is procrastination because of an intimidating target. We might want to lose eight stone but when you have only lost one pound at the end of the week, your eight stone target seems like a lifetime away and so, with dwindling motivation, your attention and dedication to your target wains. It is the same for revising for an exam or reading a large book: we are not especially good at focusing on the positive things, the weight you have lost or the amount you have read, or the closer you are to your sales target. However, we are very good at focusing on the intimidating chasm between where you are and where you want to be. However, if you were to practice the piano just ten percent more than you did currently, your playing would improve. If you aimed for just a ten percent uplift in sales, it could mean a huge difference to your bottom line. Likewise, a ten percent reduction in costs or waste could make a huge difference, too. It could be the solution to preventing redundancies. Ten percent is such a tiny, almost insignificant amount, it is easily overlooked. After all, in most other areas, ten percent is ignored. Certainly in sales or in discount offers, we are more interested and attracted to fifty percent discounts or seventy five percent sales, or even twenty five percent. The days of ten percent attracting anyone's attention are long gone. When I explain to business leaders that we are going to aim to improve output by ten percent, they often challenge me: "but we were thinking something more like eighty percent?" The problem with setting such a huge jump as the initial target is that so many people fall massively short. An interesting thing happens when we set ourselves an easily achievable goal: many people don't even attempt to try it because it is almost so obvious that it could be done, that it does not provide sufficient motivation to do it. Similarly, if a target or goal appears to be too unrealistically obtainable, we do not attempt that either. The secret to goal setting and changing our behaviour is to set clearly defined, realistic goals, which is why the +10% Principle is just so effective.

As Barrie says: "the principle can have an immediate and profound impact on both organisations and individuals and can be used by first-line supervisors, sales managers, newspaper editors, hospital administrators, top level executives, school principals, ministers, university presidents, athletic coaches, government leaders, teachers, choir conductors and anyone else interested in high performance." In most human organisations, the difference between ordinary and extraordinary is often just a tiny amount. It can be just a few small changes that will enable significant results. Yet in other areas of life, the gap between ordinary and extraordinary is often huge. Barrie tells the story of when he sailed on a small boat to see Mount Rainier, an icon of the Washington landscape which stands some 14,410 feet above sea level at its peak. In this tiny boat on Puget Sound, he looks up at the looming mountain range and although each of the mountains are all tall and mighty in their own right, Mount Rainier's colossal size makes the rest of the range seem tiny in comparison. The difference between the other mountains and Mount Rainier is not a mere ten percent; it is huge. Talk to him for long enough and Barrie will also tell you of his trip to the Sears Tower in Chicago. From the tower's viewing gallery, on the one hundred and tenth floor, if you look out across the city, you can see for thirty miles or more if the day is a clear one. Look down and it appears as though you are looking at miniatures. Barrie says that even the other towers like the Lincoln Tower look like toys because the Sears Tower is so tall. Yet if you stand on the street outside the Lincoln Tower and crick your neck to look up; it looks enormous. I experienced the same thing when I was working in New York a few years ago, looking out from the Empire State building; the difference between ordinary and extraordinary is a huge differential.

Yet when it comes to the organisations themselves, the difference between the ordinary ones and the extraordinary ones is nowhere near like the difference between Mount Rainier and the other mountains. As Barrie so eloquently describes: "the difference between being a run-of-the-mill organisation and a high-performing one is a small increment." Just ten percent. If you look around you and consider the interactions with organisations you've had recently, how many would you grade as extraordinary or outstanding? The reality is that most people work for organisations producing average results that deliver average services. Most of us receive an average wage for an average day's work. This is not necessarily unacceptable to us but few of us or the organisations we connect with are extraordinary. But what if every teacher in your local school vowed to improve just one course by ten percent for the next academic year? What if your local police force found ways to reduce just violent crimes, not all crimes, just violent ones, by ten percent? What if your local hospital found a way to reduce laboratory costs by ten percent? What if a leading manufacturing company could cut the production lead-time on just one product by ten percent? What if that manufacturing company was a pharmaceutical company? What if every parent committed to spending just ten percent more time with their children?

Agreeing in principle or with a sentiment that sits well with us morally is one thing. However, when faced with choices, we all behave quite differently. For example, if a new local bakery opened just down the road from you, (as it has from me), and it sold freshly baked produce that were ten percent better quality and tastier than those sold where you usually shop, would you consider shopping at the new bakery? If the staff at the new bakery welcomed you by your name, were polite and carefully wrapped the goods you bought in a nice cardboard box, would that make a difference? Would you consider moving your children to a different school if they could improve the competence or self-confidence of your children by ten percent? What about if your bank offered you a ten percent better return on your investment than who you currently bank with? Would you change banks? Would you pay thirty percent more to be ten percent more attractive? Just a ten percent difference can make a huge impact. No matter whether a business is large or small, if it lost ten percent of its business and did not replace it, this would have an impact across the board yet conversely most businesses can and readily would handle an increase in customers of ten percent.

Where the +10% Principle really comes into its own, however, is when combined with Vilfredo Pareto's principle of the vital few. Pareto was an Italian economist and sociologist who discovered that for most manufacturing firms, just a small amount of their inventory, less than ten percent, accounted for some ninety percent of the total value of their inventory. Look around you at home or even at work; it is the same for us, too. Most of us own literally hundreds if not thousands of items, from clothes and books to cutlery and furniture, yet it is our homes, cars and savings that account for ninety percent of our net worth. Unless you are my Mother, in which case the value of the shoe collection way surpasses any other material objects owned. So when I announce that we are going to aim to change or improve just a small amount, leadership teams look at me like I have been drinking de-icer and I explain that we really don't need to be better at everything in order to be extraordinary. High performance is within all of our reach.

Plasticity

Thankfully, science has moved on. I say thankfully because it was not all that long ago when the general consensus in the scientific community was that whatever we learnt was effectively ingrained into our brains for the rest of our lives. Once it was learnt, it could not be unlearnt and presumably that made people who were especially skilled at playing the piano, for example, feel quite relieved but for those with unsavoury habits I can only imagine that they lived their lives mortified, confined by the notion of having an incurable brain problem. The belief that the neural network was concrete, made concepts of behaviour change difficult, understandably. The concept of plasticity is just one of the results of the scientific community developing and moving on, although there is still some resistance to some of the ideas presented. Plasticity is presented as the brain's lifelong ability, (and that is quite key), to reorganise itself based on new experiences. So at any given moment, we only think we know what we know. But what we really know is what we can recall and it is that recall which is determined by what we have learned and how we have learnt it.

Neuroplasticity is the term given to the concept that a brain can in fact change. In essence it is an understanding of the brain's ability to change its own structure and functions through thought and activity. It provides a scientific insight into the centuries old mantra: what we think, we become. For example, if certain areas of the brain failed for whatever reason, due to illness or injury, then other parts of the brain could sometimes take over. This advancement developed from teams of scientists who had observed that children would not always be stuck with the mental abilities they are born with; that damaged brains can often reorganise themselves, having one part of the brain substitute for another part that has failed and, incredibly, one of these scientists also discovered that learning, thinking and acting can turn our genes on or off, therefore, shaping our brain's anatomy and our own behaviour. Professor Norman Doidge suggests that this could well be "one of the most extraordinary discoveries of the twentieth century." However, Doidge warns that it isn't necessarily all good news: "[plasticity] renders our brains not only more resourceful but also more vulnerable to outside influences." Neuroplasticity is the reason, should you need one, why you can (and should), change your mind. It offers an explanation for, and scientific permission, to think differently and be, within reasonable realistic constraints, whatever we wish to be. The concept of neuroplasticity is regarded as the reason why scientists have been able to teach people who have been blind since birth to see, the deaf to hear and for victims of debilitating stroke, to recover. I know it sounds like the stuff of fantasy and to go into great detail is beyond the scope of this book but I'd highly recommend grabbing a copy of Doidge's book *The Brain That Changes Itself*; it's a compelling read.

The part that is perhaps most useful for the context here, is not the remarkable stories of how the brain has helped people to overcome physical challenges and disabilities, but the use of plasticity as a concept to rewire the brain to assist us with obsessions, phobias, trauma - and at its most elementary - our outlook, opinion and mood. No matter where you are right now, or where your staff team are, psychologically in terms of mindset, morale or even specific behaviours, we absolutely can - and I believe must - change those things. No behaviour is permanent (think about how you've changed to various brands when shopping, chosen a different route to drive to a familiar destination or even started a new hobby) and nor is any thought, opinion or emotion. Each morning when I wake up, I choose happy and I choose positive. Admittedly that isn't always easy, especially not when the dark knight of depression plays its hand. However, to allow ourselves to act in any way in which we are not completely comfortable and 100% happy with; that does not reflect our morals and ethical values, for example, is an example of how outside influences can shape us to become something that is not necessarily representative of who we truly are. If nothing else, plasticity helps us to understand just how fragile the stability of our mind is and how easily it is both influenced and corrected.

Choice Blindness

It is not so much the choices themselves that we make but the repercussions and consequences of those choices that affect our lives and the lives of others. Which is why better understanding what is involved in making the choices and decisions that we do and how to avoid some common pitfalls, which often have their own impact on our choices, is so important. Being armed with information such as this, you have the option to apply it, which in turn takes you further on your journey toward extraordinary. Many of us believe that we have free will, whereas in actual fact we don't. The thought of someone else controlling our actions or influencing the decisions we make does not sit well with many of us and the majority of us like to feel in control of our own lives, or at least believe that we are. If we really did have the free will, as so many of us assume we have, advertising and sales pitches would have no effect.

So why is it that so many of us feel that our choices feel so free and unlimited? Much of the answer lies squarely at the feet of the psychological principle 'cognitive dissonance'. When your brain holds two competing ideas, thoughts, behaviours or beliefs, it creates conflict. This conflict is termed cognitive dissonance and one common way in which your brain deals with it is to change its attitude, beliefs or behaviours in order to bring one of those competing ideas into prominence. In itself, it makes us feel as though we have made a decision freely. This is worth knowing because very often we are at the mercy of cognitive dissonance but are unaware. Have you ever made a decision about your children, perhaps that they cannot do something, only to have realised on reflection it perhaps was not the best decisions to make, or were proved wrong, but you stuck with that decision so as to be consistent for your children? Well that is cognitive dissonance. And it exists because what we think is our free will, isn't truly free. The winning decision is determined by our context and history and in fact the same thing can be said for all of our behavioural decisions: they are simply a product of our genetic and environmental history. I heard some remarkable and concerning examples of this when I attended a speed awareness course once. I had been coming home from some consultancy work in Northampton, which is apparently as well known for its confusing road layouts and speed cameras as it is for its shoe factories and shoe museum. If I was the mayor of Northampton I'd be commissioning a very good public relations team to find something else - anything - that could replace the reputation of a museum for shoes.

Traveling down a slight hill (there's always a ready justification when you listen to someone's guilty speeding story), the speed camera snapped me traveling at thirty three miles per hour in a thirty mile per hour limit zone. It is my first and as it stands only speeding offence. However, the faceless group who issue the letter, offering you the choice to attend a four hour speed awareness course or pay a fine, seem not to care that I once saved several lives when I stopped at a major incident on the M1. Or perhaps they don't know. Either way, I opted for the speed awareness course and the thought of a severe telling off lasting four hours was not helping me sleep. I imagined a clumsy, jumped up jobs-worth police officer who had been removed from main policing duties to the relief of his colleagues, probably due to a level of ineptitude or incompetence, let loose on members of the public caught speeding. I replayed the image I'd created in my mind of four hours of tutting, shaking their head at me and making me feel really small to see if they could push me to tears. Only, it didn't turn out quite like that, thankfully. Barry and June, the instructors, were quite charming. I was so relieved when they started by saying that they were not, in fact, here to berate us for four hours; simply educate us.

I honestly don't remember much about the course, which I am a little reluctant to offer publicly in case I get hauled in for another round. However, the truth is, having passed an advanced driving assessment and been trained in response driving, I actually knew all of the answers to June and Barry's questions. I, genuinely, was caught a few miles per hour over the limit due to a momentary lapse of speed judgement as the pitch of the road changed. I know, I know, I can hear you straining from here: I was still speeding though. There are only three parts of the course I remember well and one of them was when Barry showed a series of photographs of roads: a dual carriageway, a high street and a country road. Our task was simple - to answer his question: "What is the speed limit on this road?" I remember at the time thinking this four hour course was going to be a walk in the park. What happened next, however, made my mouth spontaneously fall open. As Frankie Howerd would say: "my gast was well and truly flabbered."

In response to the photo of the dual carriageway that Barry projected, the answers that were offered by the other twenty five or so attendees, ranged from "fifty" and "seventy five" to "ninety miles per hour." Now these were not young, inexperienced drivers. The majority of my fellow pedal heavy drivers were lorry drivers, with a few taxi and delivery drivers sprinkled in there, too. These were, in effect, professional drivers who were, frankly, making up speed limits! The speed limit in the UK is seventy miles per hour. It always has been! It has never been more than that. And where on earth did that one man get the extra five miles per hour from to qualify seventy five miles per hour?! Yet over the course of time, presumably by driving at these exaggerated speeds, they have normalised these numbers in their mind. The power of cognitive dissonance saw them adopt the, entirely fabricated, speed limits in their mind, which resulted in them sitting in on a speed awareness course, presumably protesting the whole way there that they knew the speed limits. In case you are at all interested - and if you aren't, I am going to tell you anyway; I got one hundred percent in the speed test, full marks for me on that part. I know my speeds. Give or take three miles per hour. All of us fall victim to this choice blindness from time to time, which is exactly why we need to question our decisions more and fully understand the choices we make, supported by fact or the very best information available at the time. Take a moment to look around you though and you quickly realise that very many, dare I say most, do not behave in this way: they take information at face value. Someone has said something to them and they then continue to offer this information, entirely unchecked, to everyone who will listen. You read something in a magazine or newspaper and accept it as gospel, despite the lack of evidence or balanced information and you then proceed to repeat what you have read as a given factual statement. My Mother is especially guilty of this. I remember driving past some road-works, which were unattended and obviously had been each time my Mother had driven past because she said, in quite a frustrated tone: "Well that's typical isn't it; no workmen. They're never there. They're probably drinking tea somewhere and still getting paid." I remember thinking at the time that this seemed like quite a generalised, sweeping statement to make, so I offered an alternative: "Well, just because they aren't there, it doesn't mean they are actively avoiding work." Mother was not accepting that as a valid response: "Well then why put the road-works up? It's ridiculous. It's an inconvenience and when they are there they just drink tea all day." All day? They drink tea all day? What if the company responsible for the road works are waiting for a part or a piece of equipment? What if they are only permitted to work at night when the road is quieter? What if the once or twice you have driven past you happened to do so when they were taking a break from all of the work you didn't happen to see? Some may say I am clearly optimistic, pragmatic and practical. I would probably agree. However, this mentality of 'ask no questions' is very commonplace. It is, in effect, ordinary. One of the purposes of Be a Purple Banana is to challenge this blindness to choices available to us, which could assist us in forming more educated and useful opinions, which in turn help us to live a life less ordinary and make a difference to our lives and those of the people we lead, teach, treat, help, serve or assist.

Interviewing and researching individuals for this book who are extraordinary or who have achieved extraordinary things raised some fascinating commonalities. For example, many of those people who others deemed extraordinary or to have done extraordinary acts refused to accept situations as given. They either believed that something else could be done or that there was another way or that things would change in the future. They also appeared to question a lot, too. They asked "why?" or "how can we improve this?"; "how can we change this?" It is through questioning ourselves and other people: our beliefs, our thoughts, our behaviours, that we can not only better understand why we do the things we do and how to change them for the better, but to quite literally train our brain to think differently. And if we all took time to question more, it is not only ourselves that would, in turn, become better people but those around us, too.

CHAPTER 4

THE EXTRAORDINARY HOW-TO

"For of all sad words of tongue
or pen, the saddest are these:
it might have been."

John Greenleaf Whittier, influential American Quaker poet
and ardent advocate of the abolition of slavery.

Keeping It Going

While my Mum was in High Wycombe Hospital more than thirty years ago, giving birth to me, my Grandma was walking down the hill which their house was built on. As an allegedly chubby child (personally I never saw it but then I did love cake - and still do), Grandma would often take me to the vast expanse of green park opposite their house, to kick around a ball in her attempt to get me exercising. However, she continued to bake the most delicious cakes. As Grandma was walking down the hill, she was struck with a crippling pain, which she described as feeling like labour pains. Unbeknownst to anyone at the time, it was at the same time that my Mum was giving birth to me. I didn't know that until recently, but it is interesting to think that she experienced an unexplained sympathetic pain similar to my Mother's, at allegedly the same time. Fast forward over thirty years and as I was getting ready yesterday morning, I plugged the iron in, about nine o'clock in the morning, I thought of my Grandma and the sadness I would feel when she passes away. My mind was consumed with thoughts of her lying in her bed, now unable to communicate very well, not eating or drinking and being turned every two hours to avoid pressure sores by staff at the care home she is in. Her character gone. Her personality gone. Her smile and her laughter all but gone. I remember at the time thinking it was a somewhat random and intense thought to be triggered by plugging an iron in. Almost an hour later, while I was sat at my desk in my home office, my Mum called with news of my Grandma's death. She had died at almost exactly the same time I thought of her.

Her death has left a wake of devastation for me and I am sure for her children, too. I loved my Grandma dearly and as my Aunt put it so beautifully, she was such a Godly example of a woman. She was deeply religious, living her life as a model Christian and although I am a humanist, we never disagreed on anything - her concern for humanity and all living things was something I respected and identified with. Now my Grandma has gone, it makes this book so much more poignant. When memories are all that remains, it puts the fragility of life very much into perspective. Now more than ever before, I believe that far too many of us take for granted, the fact that we take life and our time alive for granted. We all know that life is comparatively short given all of the things we could and often aspire to do but we do very little about it. Often it takes shattering blows to our lives to be reminded of this fact. If we were more consciously aware of how limited and delicate our time alive is, I believe we would achieve more with our lives and we would be more positive, driven and fulfilled as a result because of that consciously active drive. My Grandma used to tell people that grass will never grow around my feet and I am told was apparently very proud of me and my achievements. Very occasionally I talk to groups of young people at business events or school leavers undecided on what direction to take their lives in. These are the rare times that I share many of my accomplishments and people are often quite surprised at just what I have achieved. I don't know why I have accomplished so much with my life but I do know that it has, in turn, fuelled my curiosity, determination to achieve, sense of happiness and positivity. At the very least, one thing I almost never experience is boredom! Perhaps that is the secret to a happy relationship; to keep one or both parties busy so that neither becomes bored? Boredom tends to stem from a lack of interest or having little or nothing to do that interests you, which in turn causes you to become irritable. When people suggest that I should slow down, or do less or just focus on one thing, I remind them of just how short life is. When did you last see a member of your family, or a certain person in your phonebook? Six months ago? Eighteen months ago? Time flies and we never get that time back so why on earth would I want to only do one thing or "take a break?" I have only seen a tiny amount of what the world has to offer. I have met just a sample of its inhabitants and come into contact with a relatively insignificant amount of just what is possible. It is time to stop putting things off and live the life you deserve to live, to stop dealing in the ordinary and to begin making extraordinary differences, extraordinary advances and extraordinary memories.

As I mentioned, my Grandma had a very strong faith; she was a dedicated Christian who believed that God had a place for her in Heaven. That thought comforted her for all of her life, knowing that everything that happened in her life was all part of the overall plan. By the time her dementia had set in, for her remaining five years, she would regularly tell us that all she wanted was to die and be with Jesus. It was heartbreaking to witness and hear and it made me realise just how important it is for us all to consider ways to improve our lives and not settle for the ordinary because when that time comes for all of us, I would hate for it to be full of what ifs and if onlys. Regret gnaws at us and as Emily Bronte so succinctly put it: "remorse is the poison of life."

Having just re-read some of what I have written in an attempt to ensure it all makes sense, you would be forgiven for thinking that the concept of being extraordinary has in itself a lot to do with being happy. I was quite clear when I set out to write this book that I did not want it to be one of those motivational, self-help, inspirational books. They make me shudder and always make me feel a little awkward. Perhaps it's the cheesiness of them or the way that they position everything as perfect and recite stories that seem far too good to be true and most likely aren't. However, I suppose I just can't avoid that category, to an extent. I hope this book doesn't read like some of those self-righteous books but if it does I apologise. You see the notion of being a purple banana is indeed about changing behaviour, which is the core thread of many self-help books. In that way at least, there is a similarity. However, the reason that the subject of happiness does feature in this book, either as a product of being extraordinary, thinking extraordinarily and doing extraordinary things, or of behavioural characteristic in order to achieve the extraordinary, is two-fold. Firstly, somewhat selfishly I admit, it is easier to type "happy" and for you to grasp what that means as an example of an appealing, positive emotional response and state. I will not attempt to define happy here, but if we can agree that in the context of this book at least, it includes the feeling of contentedness, cheerfulness and enjoyment. Is that okay? However, the main reason for using the term "happy" is that happiness is the root, the main driver, for most of our actions, life decisions and dreams. How do we know this? Well, there is a very simple test that you can do with yourself now and indeed with anyone else - I will assume you choose a friend or colleague rather than simply grabbing the person sat next to you if you are reading this on a train or in a coffee shop. It has just dawned on me the power I may have by writing this. Anyway, to highlight how it works, ask yourself what your dream is: what you are determined to do. For example you might answer: "I want to move to a third world country and help prevent world hunger." You might respond: "I want to be rich." Whatever answer you give, ask yourself "why?" For each new answer you give, again ask yourself "why?" It will really push you and anyone you ask, to think about what it is that is driving these dreams, choices and behaviours you have or have the desire for. Eventually, in nearly every case, you will reply to "why?" with: "to be happy."

Happiness

I was talking about this very thing to a colleague of mine, Terry Gormley recently. Terry, like me, coaches individuals and teams, however, where my clients are mostly from all areas of business, Terry works a lot with sports people. He was asked to speak with a team of rugby players in order to assist them with focus and their behaviour on the pitch. One of the players was especially rowdy and causing a few problems with shouting out and showing off in front of his fellow team mates. One thing you should always avoid when working with psychologists, behaviourists or good coaches is being a wally. Any behaviour that is not naturally your own, we can spot from the second we lay eyes on you. We can sniff out unnaturalness like a pig can locate truffles. That isn't an especially good analogy is it? Like a wolf can smell lamb. Anyway you get my point. So, naturally, Terry has singled out this one individual as being a bit of a wally. Terry asks him: "why do you play rugby?" To which he flippantly answers: "for the money!" to the cheers and jeers of his team mates. Terry looked at him and said: "no you don't." This response caused an increase in the surging flow of testosterone in the rugby player, if there was indeed any more that could be leaked. "Yes I do" came the reply. "You don't" said Terry, "You don't play rugby for the money, so why do you play it?" The rugby player, now glaring at Terry responded again: "yes. I. do." Terry changed tact: "okay, what do you do with the money you earn?" The player thought momentarily and replied with: "I buy nice things for my wife and daughter." "And by buying nice things for your wife and daughter, what does that do to them?" The player considered this, furrowing his eyebrows. "It makes them happy." "Exactly," said Terry, "you play rugby because it makes your wife and your daughter happy and in turn that makes you happy."

The quest for happiness is at the very core of most of our decisions and choices. Think about that because it is critically important to a better understanding not only of your own behaviour, but that of others, too. Why is it that you bought a new sofa? You may well answer with practical reasons: "The other one was old and I was fed up with the mice that had burrowed into it" or "we needed a new one." However, no matter what practical reasons you offer, at the very root is the fact that buying a new sofa would make you happier. It may well be that you find happiness through greater comfort or the absence of the smell of mouse urine, but nonetheless, happiness is the driver. What about the reasons we end relationships? Again, you might offer practical reasons that are at the forefront of your mind: "I couldn't stand the way she left the toilet seat down, drowned the house with that potent smell of nail polish and obsessively played Backstreet Boys really loudly when cleaning." The differences in musical taste and bathroom habits may well have driven you apart, but by separating, you will in turn find happiness through less intrusion into your own life preferences and habits - and you know that. You are well aware that these things are not making you happy and that by changing them, you will realise happiness. Only quite often those reasons are not readily considered and accepted; they remain within your subconscious mind. Sometimes it is the simple things that can have the biggest impact. My Grandma used to say: "smile a while and while you smile another will smile and soon there's miles and miles of smiles because you smiled." Now, to claw back any sudden disinterest you may have, allow me to explain the science behind this and exactly why happiness and more specifically, smiling, is so relevant to our journey to understanding extraordinary.

In 1989 Robert Zajonc, a social psychologist who would later become known for his work on social and cognitive processes, published one of the most significant studies ever conducted on the emotional effects of smiling. He had his participants repeat certain vowel sounds that stretched the facial muscles into a shape that mimicked that of a smile, for example they were asked to make long "e" sounds. The participants reported feeling happier after making the long "e" sound and not feeling as happy when making a long "u" sound, which forced the facial muscles into more of a pout. Zajonc took this a step further and showed some groups of participants images of facial expressions; another group were shown the images and asked to make them and yet another group were asked to make the facial expressions, while looking in a mirror. The resulting evidence suggested that smiling is a cause of happy feelings as the participant's pre-study scores into their emotional state were overwhelmingly lower than they were following the experiment, for those who used the mirror. This is because the facial muscles involved in smiling have a direct effect on certain brain activities associated with happiness. Since Zajonc's work, there have been a number of different studies and fluctuating renewed interest in the area of testing smiles and happiness. The take home message is always the same: if you are having a bad day or you need to feel happier, begin by smiling because there appears to be a converse relationship with smiling and happiness - smiling causes happiness but happiness causes smiling. Admittedly, if you have lost your wallet and your mobile phone, it's unlikely that smiling is going to make you feel any better about it, let alone happy. However, for the purposes of our journey into understanding how we can apply the principles of being extraordinary in our role, our places of work and indeed our life, it is a powerful tool to be aware of.

Hiding from Happiness

It is interesting how so many people don't mention happiness specifically and readily, as a reasoning for their choices, behaviours and actions. It is almost as though they are unaware that it is this perpetual search for happiness that is driving them. Or perhaps it is a general feeling that there should be something more practical that should be the reasoning, rather than something as potentially "fluffy" as happiness. Maybe it is a British thing; we do tend to be a bit stiff and reserved when it comes to displaying and discussing our emotions. Certainly the exercise of challenging your answers with "why?" seems to highlight that, as you will discover if you do it, a lot of people when questioned with "why?" respond with: "well, I guess it's to be happy?" So what relevance does this have to making the step-change from ordinary to extraordinary? Well, if you understand that happiness is what you and most other people are ultimately searching for, it makes it much easier to make the correct decisions and choices - and indeed create extraordinary things for you and those around you that are much more likely to be successful, or at the very least, accepted more readily. If it helps or goes a part towards making someone happy or at the very least experience happiness, all-be-it momentarily, it is highly likely to not only be a success but also sit as out of the ordinary. The notion of being a purple banana takes on a whole new meaning when you consider this.

Embracing the notion of striving to be extraordinary does not bring with it a long time scale or a struggle to have a research thesis published or accepted by a club or association; at its most basic, it can simply be about creating moments of happiness because as we have seen, those will be appreciated and have the greatest impact with most people. When I am invited to speak to organisations, I often refer to how customers have an imaginary sign around their neck, which, if it wasn't imaginary and one could see, would say: 'Make Me Feel Special' because that is ultimately what every customer is looking for. Who wouldn't choose to shop somewhere that made them feel special, over another business that offered the same product or service? However, the big revelation is that it is not just customers who wear this imaginary sign. We all do. Children have it and teachers need to know that. Your spouse has it and you need to know that. Patients have it; prospects have it - we all wear the sign that asks for us to be made to feel special because it is an innate human desire. You might well be tempted to ask: "how do you know?" After all, if the sign is imaginary, how do I know what your sign says? It might read 'drug free since March', or 'private sign: do not read'. However, I imagined the imaginary sign in question, so my imagination makes the rules in this case. Okay? Now if you can strive to achieve making someone feel special, it is highly likely, by default, that you will have connected at an emotional level with that individual and in the case of a customer, gone a long way to securing repeat custom and a long-term relationship with them. In the case of a teacher and a student, you will have instantly built trust and cemented a stronger channel of communication. It is because of an understanding of this inane human desire to be made to feel valued, respected and wanted that so many stories exist from people raving about great customer service, or a fantastic restaurant your friend went to, or the way you were treated in hospital, or a product someone bought, or a favourite teacher at school - because these are recollections of interactions with people and experiences that made those people feel special in some way. They stood out as positive examples for the people involved and as a result, they get recounted. These people were, for them, purple bananas.

It is, I think, quite charming that many of our actions can have the side effect of creating happiness for others. I believe that happiness is a side effect of many things we do in life, however, it's very seldom used as a primary objective. You don't all that often hear someone say: "we'll do this to make our customers happy" or "let's do this; it'll really make our someone happy." While that isn't necessarily a bad thing, I do think that being more consciously aware of the impact our actions can have is critical to our greater success in life. After all, if sending a hand-written thank you card can help turn a customer into a loyal fan of your organisation and randomly sending someone a bunch of flowers to thank them for their efforts can make someone's day, should we perhaps not be considering the impact we can have on more people, more often? And if we acknowledge that we can have such an impact on other people (and ourselves), should we be doing something more about it? However, it is not solely because these acts are not every-day, ordinary occurrences as to why people are seen to be extraordinary when they carry them out but that the acts are unexpected and appeal to that imaginary sign we are all wearing.

Chemicals

If I say oxytocin, you will probably recognise it from school biology lessons or indeed from the media. It's a neuropeptide (which essentially means it acts as a neurotransmitter, so has an impact on the brain, but looks a certain way) that is sometimes referred to as "the cuddle hormone" or "the moral molecule." I know, science sometimes doesn't help itself, does it? It's produced in the hypothalamus, which is the slightly hidden bit that looks a little like a tooth, and then stored and secreted by the pituitary gland (for the biology nuts reading this, you'll remember it's specifically the one at the back, the posterior pituitary gland). It is most commonly discussed in relation to new mothers because during childbirth and breastfeeding there is a surge of oxytocin in the mother's body and as a result it helps the mother develop a greater 'mothering instinct': literally to decide whether to care for her child when it develops a snotty nose, for example, or throw it away. That's commonly where our understanding of oxytocin comes from. However, scientists went on to discover that oxytocin plays a role in all sorts of occasions of happiness; from helping us to recognise faces at a party and attribute the correct emotion to that face (think recognising a good friend versus recognising an ex who turned out to be the anti-Christ), to achieving orgasm (possibly with someone you met at the same party - I don't know you so I don't know your morals but if you only just met them and you're skipping to third base already? Come on now).

Now, for me and many others in the behaviour, psychology and science fields, oxytocin actually plays a much more interesting role than simply the perhaps slightly more fluffy popular portrayal of being a bonding hormone. And this is where it should also get interesting for you, too. You'll remember Zak and the pigeon drop experiment from just a few pages before and hopefully you'll recall that oxytocin plays a role in whether we trust people or not. It has also been shown to influence whether we go along with the decisions of a group or not, actually enhancing conformity. While all this talk of oxytocin may have you wanting to reach for the internet and find out how you can have it pumped around your office and bottling it for those plug-in diffusers, you might want to bare with me just a few more sentences longer because several experiments have suggested that while oxytocin makes us more generous and trusting, it doesn't actually make us any more gullible. For example, if you have evidence that you are being lied to or if something doesn't quite sit right with you, no matter how much oxytocin is flooding your brain, you will still be able to withdraw trust. We are all still consciously able to terminate a relationship or remove our involvement from a situation if we feel our best interests aren't at heart. While this might be reassuring, the final twist in the oxytocin tale is that while we can control its effects on our behaviour, if there is conflicting information to how we feel as a result of it, we really can get quite carried away by its effects to the contrary. Humans are social creatures and largely we enjoy being a part of a group;

that's one of the many reasons why team activities work so well in the workplace. However, considering all of the research, it suggests that we like being a part of a group so much that we'd actually be willing to hurt others in order to stay in that group and continue enjoying that feeling of collaboration. The desire to belong is commonly considered to compromise our ethical and empathic instincts. In other words, if we let ourselves get carried away, we could well end up in an environment that prevents us from being virtuous. We really do need to be consciously aware of our behaviour, rather than simply allowing ourselves to follow the crowd if extraordinary is to remain in our reach. That's one of the key attributes I believe to creating extraordinary people: by all means follow the crowd and do as others do, but remain consciously aware of why you're there. Follow with purpose.

Drama

Sometimes we all get a little hung up in the moment: stress focuses us too tightly on one tiny little thing, or a wave of self-importance makes us ignore everyone else around us – or you drop something, it breaks and then you become angry and possibly even tearful. Someone I know is a designer and she dropped an orange mug. It was not just her favourite mug, presumably because it made coffee taste somehow better than any other mug, but it was a special type of orange, too. I think only a designer would notice something like that. However, when she dropped it and it broke, it created double the tragedy and to this day, if anyone carelessly mentions the mug incident of 2013, it sends her spiralling into a series of much publicised self-pitying behaviours. We can all identify with those moments in life where we become so wrapped up in what is essentially something of little to no consequence in the grand scheme of things – a non-problem if you will. Admittedly, at the time it can be all-consuming, but many people just cannot seem to help themselves: their dramatic reaction is automatic. It is all around us in road rage, queues, internet forums and at home; in all of these areas we experience people who appear to lose the ability to maintain rational thought. The smashed glass no longer matters; it is beyond repair and so moving forwards we should replace it or move on. My Grandma used to say: "no point crying over spilt milk." Neither is there any point in crying over the selfish person who was in a rush and cut you up, or the arrogant shop salesperson. For all of the time you spend concentrating on the negative things, consumed by the things that have gone wrong, you are no different than the very people that annoyed you. We do seem to have a strange predisposition as a species to not be especially realistic in our reasoning. It is little wonder where the term 'arm chair philosopher' came from when I watch a reality television show with people casting accusations and assumptions as the news broadcasts on their television, or having a twitch at the net curtains and revealing an opinion about where the person has been, where they are going or passing judgement on their life. What absolutely fascinates me is how so many people manage to successfully pass off their opinion of something, of which they seemingly know nothing about, as fact!

Many years ago when I was working in healthcare, I remember holding the hand of a dying man called Frank. He had terminal throat cancer and was especially kind natured and selflessly thoughtful; one of those people you meet and wish you'd known for longer than you have. He was old by the time I met him; I can't remember exactly how old but late seventies, I imagine. Frank's wife held tightly onto one of his hands and I gently held the other. Frank looked at me with his glassy, steely blue eyes and said in his slightly gruff voice, with a sombre hint that he knew exactly what was coming: "no one lives forever." Frank died just a week or so following that. For the rest of my life I shall remember that moment and how it almost instantly put everything before, then and forevermore into perspective: the time I shouted and swore at a car that had cut me up; how angry and irritable I'd got when I smashed my own favourite mug; when I was running really late for a friend's wedding and ruined the rest of the day for myself because I was so stressed and flustered. Thankfully, as Buck's Fizz popularised, those days are gone. For me, it was largely because of that moment with Frank: it took that meeting for me to appreciate that all of the things that had happened to me in life up until that moment had passed me by. They'd just happened to me. Of course there were many really wonderful times, memorable achievements and the occasional sad time, too. However, I had my head down and was getting on with my life, seemingly like most of us. I see this everywhere I go – very little appreciation of the fragile and finite properties of life. We are here but once, yet the way people move around you would be forgiven for thinking that this was merely a rehearsal and that we will get to do it all over again, playing out those parts we didn't quite get right with a renewed vigour, flamboyance or tact that we failed on the first time around. It was about this time, when I met Frank, that I recalled my experience, stood in a town centre watching the ant. It occurred to me, stronger than ever before, that not always doing what is considered normal; making an effort to reach for something more than just the ordinary, was the key to being successful in business; finding happiness; creating memorable moments for others and being better teachers, nurses, directors, parents or indeed people. We can all perform at a greater level and create a more significant impact when we ask ourselves: "why?" Fellow TED speaker, Sir Ken Robinson, challenges why schools teach in restricting time tables, which force students to choose topics of study they may not necessarily like, nor that make the most of their individual abilities. Why do we invite armchair philosophers, with no legal training, onto a jury to make unqualified opinions? Why do religions that support love cause so many wars? Why are you, you? Why do hose pipes kink at the opposite end to where you end up, even when there wasn't a kink there before? I put that last one in because it always puzzles me. We should questions ourselves more: our thoughts, our behaviours, our beliefs.

Doing Nothing

I am certainly not suggesting that we question the status quo in order to go against the grain or be intentionally obstructive, however, a lot of things just happen to us in life, which we do not consider. Without consideration how can we create a platform for and embrace creativity? Everything will remain constant without our ability to ask "why?" Some of us will step out of our front door one day and never come home. Our plans for next month won't matter if we don't even get a tomorrow. It's all too easy to become wholly consumed with what we are doing, without appreciating that one day, it will all be over and all that will be left are thousands of things on our 'to do' list that we never got round to doing. If you do nothing, nothing will happen. It is the safest and easiest place to be but it is possibly also the least interesting, offering the least variety and certainly is not the formula for doing anything extraordinary. No one ever became extraordinary, make an extraordinary impact or did extraordinary things by not doing anything differently. There is nothing extraordinary about ordinary. So the first part of our journey to extraordinary things begins with us. We simply cannot simultaneously keep one foot on where we are now and make a step towards where we want to be or what we want to do. We would never feel fully committed so making that step is simply the start of the process. If people can rebuild their lives from the lowest point of homelessness, with not a single penny to their name, then you can easily correct something that goes wrong, too. In many ways it is simply a matter of mindset: those things we believe we can do, we do and those things we don't believe we can do, we don't.

Waking Up

If you were to take just a few minutes now to put this book down and think, or perhaps just let your mind wander as you hold the book in front of you, to reassess what gets you up in the morning, it may provide you with a reminder of the one thing you should keep in mind more often: the very reason you get up and live your life. Many parents keep a photo of their child in their wallets and lovers keep their respective sweetheart's photo in a locket for very much the same reasons: these reminders of better things worthwhile spur you on when the going gets tough or when despondency sets in. They help to focus the mind and act as reminders of why you are sat in front of a computer writing a book at a quarter past midnight.

But just why do you get up in the morning? Have you ever considered that before? Is it to earn as much money as possible? Is it to enjoy life and see what new things you can learn today? Is it to further yourself up the career ladder you have chosen? It may be to make full use of the time you are alive, in appreciation of the opportunities you have. Perhaps it is to help others or make a difference in the world. Whatever your very personal reasoning for getting out of bed may be, it is worth taking the time to reassess it: does it help you to live a life more extraordinary? Does it do anything to change the ordinary into the extraordinary? Could you find a more compelling reason? My friend and colleague Dr. Ian Dunbar wakes up each morning, moves both arms, moves both legs, takes a deep breath in and if all works as expected, he says: "thank you," before getting out of bed to start his day. It is a sobering reminder of our vulnerability and dependence on our health.

Passion

If you have ever experienced that internal yearning, the "itchy feet" or unsettled sensation to seek something more, then at that precise moment in time you were, probably unknowingly, at the very beginning of your journey to becoming a purple banana. For that is how it must begin: you must have a desire to do something differently or in a way improved, or a wanting for something more. Obviously, without that desire to change what you do or the way in which you do it, there is no catalyst for that change. However, the real secret to taking ordinary people and making them extraordinary is passion. There must exist a passion within the individuals, for what they need to change. Without passion we lack interest, commitment and motivation.

I remember when I was younger I became fascinated with magic tricks, an obsession that was nurtured by my family. It wasn't necessarily the methods of the tricks themselves which were of interest to me, although the scientific part of my brain loved to discover the various modus operandi; it was peoples' reactions to the performances and discovering techniques such as misdirection, which have their methodology deeply rooted in psychology, which fascinated me the most. When I was very young I would stay with my Father's parents, or Nan and Grampy as they were known to me. My Grampy would take me for a drive and at one point, would mumble some magic words and produce a real fairground around the very next corner. If it wasn't fairgrounds it was Easter eggs and if there was a lack of local activities for him to take the credit for conjuring up, a coin would be plucked from behind my ear. I was equally happy with that, which shows just how easy going I must have been as a child. Fast forward ten years or so and I would happily get up early for school, come home and spend hours reading magic books way into the early hours of the morning. The early alarm to get up and ready for another day at school didn't seem to deter me in any way. It was the same for some of my friends at school who were musicians (Waddesdon Church of England School had a particularly worthy reputation as a school that championed the arts) and would be out until the early hours of the morning practicing their guitars or playing in bands. With passion comes an endless energy, enthusiasm and motivation to spend most of your waking hours immersed in it. It is highly likely, although not exclusive, that you are passionate about the very thing you want to change or do. That would be logical. However, if that isn't the case and you are seeking to be extraordinary at a particular subject or topic, or in terms of character and you aren't in fact passionate about it, it is quite likely that you will struggle. However, that doesn't make it impossible you understand.

We often find ourselves impassioned by the actions of others which interest, inspire or impress us, which in turn motivates us to do something similar ourselves. Only, when we begin, we frequently compare our chapter one with someone else's chapter twenty five, which is not only fantastically frustrating but demoralising, too. We're guilty, too, of not reinforcing the things we want to see more of in ourselves and in others. We're very quick to punish the things we want to see less of: children drawing on walls, dogs urinating on carpets, colleagues missing deadlines. We're not necessarily any good at punishment but we all like to think we are and are very prompt in handing it out. However, the element that has the biggest impact on our behaviour and that of others, is reinforcement. It's sad then that we're largely very poor at immediate marking and reinforcing of the behaviours we want to see more of. When people hand in their work on time, or choose paper instead of walls, or the dog chooses grass instead of carpet, we often take it for granted that things are happening as we envisaged, with little to no feedback. It is critical that we let others know when they do the right things and reinforce the behaviours we want to see more of. For example, why do so many people enjoy giving gifts? Their actions of buying the gifts, wrapping them and giving them are reinforced by the delight of the recipient and the feeling of reflected pleasure. Which is exactly why when you receive socks for Christmas or a gift you don't like, you shouldn't fake excitement or pleasure because you're setting yourself up for a lifetime of similar gifts. Which brings me to my point: the very thing you use to reinforce behaviour; to encourage it to happen again, must be reinforcing for the other person. For example, I don't drink alcohol, so if you were to thank me for doing something for you by giving me a case of Champagne, it wouldn't actively encourage me to repeat that behaviour. If you gave me book tokens, however, I'd be all over you like an aggressive rash. So, if you're looking to encourage people to do more of something, or repeat a behaviour, it is essential that you find out what they find reinforcing. You might well want to reward the team who complete the most sales, for example, and you might think that an all-expenses trip to Las Vegas would be flashy, attractive and reinforcing enough to encourage everyone to pull out all the stops and perform over and above and then to sustain that for the benefit of the company. As glitzy and attractive a trip to Las Vegas may be, it might not be as reinforcing for someone with children as having a half a day off of work, or to leave work an hour early so that they can pick their children up from school, however. Reinforcement is relative, which is exactly why some of us don't need alcohol or heroin. First find out what motivates, inspires and drives people so that you can reinforce appropriately. Do they eat chocolate or even especially like it? If not, it's a fairly empty gesture buying them a bar of chocolate to thank them for their efforts.

We can reinforce ourselves, too, by reserving those things we will work for; the things that we will look forward to, such as a bar of your favourite chocolate, a slice of that cake you made at the weekend or a cup of hot tea - or stopping work early to pick your children up from school. Rather than having these things available all of the time, reserve them for when you have completed a task, for example. Although do make sure someone else is picking the children up from school if you're not. My point is: to reinforce your focus or hard work with something you enjoy and it will help you to see more of it.

Regardless of whether you work with a team of people or not, setting up a binary feedback system is really important to share best practice and discover how other people are thinking and feeling. Those other people could be your customers, your colleagues, your students, your patients, your staff - or even your suppliers. Over the last ten years of working with some of the largest global organisations as a behaviour change consultant, one thing has repeatedly surprised me; the lack of feedback systems in place in nearly all of those organisations. And that's not an exaggeration because my Dad told me at least a million times as a child not to exaggerate. Many had customer opinion surveys and some even had staff opinion surveys; the problem with many of those is that they ran into pages, with very poor, if any, reinforcement for completing them. We've all been in the position of starting to complete a questionnaire or survey, with all the best intentions, only to get bored by question 8 when we result to just ticking random answers or answering "excellent" for the remaining ones. There are strategies to use to ensure you get reliable, high quality information fed back to you - and multiple paged surveys are not one of them! Efficacious feedback loops are continual; not periodical. Think about that for a moment. If you were burnt by an iron just the once; the very first time you touched it when it was on, you would naturally be wary of it and stay away. However, over time, your repulsion would wane and eventually you would accidentally brush past it or catch your arm on it as you manipulated the clothing you were ironing, for example. If you were not burnt by that iron regularly, every time you touched it, your understanding of when it was safe to touch and when it wasn't would be disrupted because of the unclear feedback you received. Consider a child at school. They are praised for putting in extra effort and really trying to complete all of the work in their maths class but they find maths difficult and struggle to perform at the level of the rest of the class. The teacher praises the child for putting in the effort, writes an encouraging comment in their exercise book and completes the praise with a sticker of a gold star. The child feels fantastic and is motivated to really concentrate and try their hardest again; only the next time, the teacher ignores their efforts: no praise, no written comment - no gold star. No feedback is worse than little feedback because the individual is left to work out why there was no feedback: perhaps their best efforts were not good enough? But they really, really tried. In which case, they may as well not bother because if their best efforts receive the same feedback as their minimum efforts, why put additional time and effort in?

Box It Up

The simplest way to encourage feedback is with a suggestions box. Don't roll your eyes. Yes, it's simple and no, it's not at all technical but remember that in behaviour change, we have to build foundations: start with the very simplest of things that have a big impact. When you have an understanding of those things, then we can add more complicated forms of behaviour change but you need to have the basics in place first. Besides, I promise that within three to six weeks, you'll see a difference if you do as I say. The success of this relies on it being a continual, binary feedback loop - don't worry about the jargon; I'll explain all:

Setting up Your Continual, Binary Feedback Loop (or How to Make Suggestions Boxes Work for You)

1. Start by getting a box (I told you it was easy). Now, please don't panic over the box. It can be any box; a shoe box, empty cereal box, a packing box - it really doesn't matter. Now take a few minutes to consider what reinforcement you could offer for their time and effort: consider what individuals would find reinforcing or rewarding and perhaps offer a few alternatives; for example a case of wine or some book vouchers, or some shopping vouchers or an extra day's holiday.

2. Place the box somewhere prominent in your environment and tell everyone, ideally in a weekly meeting, what it is, where it is and why it's there (and maybe ask them not to put their rubbish or post in it). Encourage them to offer suggestions for improvements to anything at all to do with your department, organisation, service, product, environment etc.

3. Every day, make a point of going to the box and looking in it, emptying it if you need to. Don't make a big deal out of this but be seen to be taking time out to check to see if anyone has offered suggestions. If they haven't, simply walk on; don't chastise or moan about it.

4. No less than once every two weeks, collate the suggestions you've received and feed back to those who took the time to contribute, thanking them and letting them know what you're doing with the suggestions. Here's a heads up for you; you'll get some crazy, totally unrealistic ones. However, to the individual offering that suggestion, it didn't appear all that crazy (and you'll have confirmed why they aren't in a more senior position - or you'll kick yourself for promoting them). It's really important that you don't belittle any of the suggestions you receive; you want to encourage everyone's involvement in a feedback system. Let the

individuals know what will happen with their suggestion; for example if you need to discuss it with others or if right now it wouldn't be feasible but that you'll keep it in mind for when the time is right - avoid using any language or tone that suggests nothing will happen with the suggestion.

5. Consider a flip chart or board (this could be digital), which can be displayed in view of everyone, to keep everyone up to date with what has been suggested and what is happening about them.

6. Reinforce everyone's act of offering suggestions with a hand written thank you note, or even rewarding those which are especially useful or help to make a difference with something more - a packet of sweets, a coffee, a book they might like or a bunch of flowers will all be unexpected and do the trick; you don't have to be looking at big budgets to make an impact.

The binary part is in your response to their suggestions: it isn't a one way street of just expecting others to keep offering suggestions to you because if they don't see changes they will assume that nothing is being done. If you need evidence that this sort of binary feedback system works, take a walk down the cereal aisle the next time you're out shopping and look for Kellogg's Variety Packs, the eight small individual boxes of cereal. This one product is hugely successful and sold in many countries around the world and I dare say worth a significant amount to Kellogg's bottom line, although they wouldn't confirm exactly how much when I called them. If you think that the Variety Pack was the result of a clever and very expensive marketing company, you'd be wrong. If you're thinking it must be the product of an intense series of product development meetings full of company directors and consultants, you'd be wrong again. This popular and profitable product was the suggestion of Harold Muntz, the head of the Institution Division at Kellogg's in 1938. He felt it was the perfect solution for children. At home, it was simple enough to satisfy children with their vastly changing tastes because consumers could always keep several different cereals in the kitchen cupboard, however, when it came to going on holiday, precious suitcase space couldn't be taken up with large boxes of cereal. The children might grow irritable, as children do, when they had to endure long stretches of the same cereal.

I know what you're thinking: first world problems, right? Anyway, when the opportunity arose for the Kellogg's workforce to make suggestions, this Mr. Muntz suggested that smaller, individual portion sized boxes of cereal, bundled together in a variety of packs (I imagine the marketing team were up all night trying to think of a name for it), would be the ideal solution to parents' conundrums. The rest, as they say, is history.

Many people believe that they must have all the answers, especially when they find themselves in a managerial or leadership role. This is both ridiculous and futile and retards development. I practice the principle of RAVE leadership. I'm not a fan of acronyms, however, this one does seem to stick with the clients who I introduce it to. It stands for Respect Appreciate and Value Everyone: do this and you'll get much more feedback.

It Just Keeps Getting Better

Some people quit very quickly. At the first sign of a challenge or obstacle in their way, they give up. I don't mean to cause controversy, however, it is my opinion that those people who give up readily when faced with a barrier blocking their goal, didn't want the goal very much. They will often argue that they really were dedicated or that they did want to meet their sales target, or that they really did want their business to succeed, or their marriage to work but they didn't want it as badly as they thought – or perhaps wanted other people to think. That is evidenced in the very fact that they gave up. If they really did want to achieve that goal, then they would have done anything to achieve it. And that for me, in meeting hundreds of thousands of people all over the world each year, is the very thing that separates the ordinary people from the extraordinary people, or at least those who achieve things altogether less ordinary.

A principle I use a lot and encourage both individuals and businesses to use is called Stacking. The application of the principle itself yields great results but the change in mindset that is created by the understanding of the principle is also responsible for great results, directly and indirectly.

In England there is a lingerie shop called La Senza. I am reliably informed that Marks and Spencer (another trusted English institution that is as part of our national heritage as cricket, tea and bowler hats), manufacture especially good knickers. If you were to buy your knickers from Marks and Spencer, you'd walk out with them in a plastic carrier bag, fulfilling its purpose perfectly. You might, I suppose walk out with them on, if you're so inclined or if you needed a new pair in a hurry but for the purposes of this explanation, I'll assume you're carrying them in a carrier bag. However, if you were to purchase your "smalls," as older people so endearingly refer to them, from La Senza, they'd be packaged up in a cardboard bag, featuring coloured rope handles. Your goods are placed inside and then tissue paper placed into the bag, along with aromatic beads (I used to refer to them colloquially as "smelly balls," but was corrected by an ex-La Senza worker at a conference last year) and finally, the whole thing is finished off with a La Senza sticker, used to close the bag. Of course, it's all retail theatrics to make your purchase feel that little bit more luxurious and your experience all the more special. However, if your lower protective garments were only placed into the cardboard bag, it wouldn't have quite the same impact. If you were to buy your underwear and it was wrapped in tissue paper, it would be a nice touch but not all that special on its own. It is the multiple touches; the special bag, the tissue paper, the aromatic beads and the sticker, when stacked together, which have such an effect. That's where the power of the principle of stacking is: it's the sum of the overall parts, which is greater than the parts themselves, which brings me to the one and only caveat: nothing is too insignificant to be stacked. For on the back of your seemingly simple, or ridiculous or silly idea, someone else gets inspiration and from that, another idea is born from someone else and before long, you create something as special and with as much impact as the La Senza packaging. But only if that very first idea is put into practice.

What one thing could you put into place that would improve, even a tiny amount, your efficiency at work; the office morale; to get you closer to your sales target, or improve customer service, or make life at home less stressful? What small additional effort could you make toward a happier marriage, enhanced patience with your children or greater self-confidence? As the Chinese philosopher Laozi so famously said: "a journey of a thousand miles begins with a single step" but the length or distance of the journey isn't important.

Why? How? And Why?

Three questions (well, technically two as one is repeated twice, although in a different context), that are unnervingly simple, yet can make a significant impact on the way that we approach challenges, respond to opportunities, create opportunities, think, behave and adapt. These three questions (I know it's two) can help shape your ability to think differently. I appreciate that sounds a little ethereal, however, something quite amazing is happening in your brain, I dare say right now.

I am quite obsessed by the brain. It's an absolutely astounding organ, yet we pump our bodies with alcohol, tobacco and drugs, which all have a detrimental affect. I say we; I mean you – and by you, I mean a vast generalisation, not necessarily specifically you. I don't drink alcohol, nor smoke. However, if we were to conduct a functional Magnetic Resonance Imaging (fMRI) scan of your brain right now (that's the one you might have seen on television, where they lay the person flat on their back as they're slid into what looks like a giant plastic doughnut), we would be able to see, highlighted in various colours, where the activity in your brain was at any given moment. We'd be able to ask you questions, pose conundrums for you to consider and ask you to imagine things, so that we could see which areas of your brain were activated by the different tasks. Following that scan, if I were to ask you to start challenging things more often, by asking "why do we do it this way?" and to then follow that question up with another: "how can we make this better?" You would begin, very gradually, to change the way that you think. You'd begin to approach things differently. If after a period of time, say three or six months, we repeated the fMRI scan and I asked you the same questions, we'd notice changes. Your brain would be functioning differently, purely as a result of how you approach things, as a direct result of the language you'd been using. Remarkable isn't it? We have the power to literally rewire our brain's neural circuitry. If you're at all surprised, interested or gobsmacked right now, this is exactly the problem I have with the scientific community. In writing this book, it is, in truth, the beginning of a crusade to make more people aware of some of the remarkable advances and understanding in psychology and human behaviour, which seem to be rarely shared with the general public. Yet it's so important because with this level of understanding, even at a primitive level, we are better able to understand just how capable we are, how to change our behaviour and why it's important, too.

Over the past twenty or so years, so much has been learned about how we behave and it's unlocked some serious questions about human potential. For example, we now understand that our behaviour today is not concrete: who we are as a person; the things we stand for, believe in, the way that we behave and think is not permanent. This means that we could be somebody completely different in six months than who we are today. It's both enlightening and encouraging to know that we can change something as significant as the way our brain behaves. Of course, many aspects play a role in this and both accentuate and prevent this potential, whether they are genetic or environmental, for example. However, this is exactly why we should challenge things more often and ask why it is that a particular process or activity is conducted in a certain way. That question alone is useful ("why do we do it this way?") but becomes significantly more powerful when coupled with asking how the very thing you are challenging could be improved ("how can we improve it?"). These questions encourage us to find improvements and changes that will project you further towards achieving the extraordinary; different to what you achieve right now. They create a mindset whereby you are approaching things differently, looking at things differently and responding to things differently, too. They are simple, yet are a catalyst for change.

The third and final "why?" features as a reminder to seek understanding. As we know, when people understand why it is they are doing something, we receive greater levels of compliance, so it is our responsibility to ensure understanding. For example, imagine the manager of a car dealership gathers his staff together early one Monday morning and says: "Right team, this month I need you to sell twenty more cars, okay? That's twenty more cars than our usual monthly target – do you think you can do it? That's it! Great! Let's remain motivated and focused, okay? Remember, you're a tiger – now go claim your Serengeti." Now, at the end of that month, it would not at all be surprising if those additional twenty cars were not sold because no one other than the manager has any concept or tangible understanding of exactly why they are being asked to sell twenty additional cars. Conversely, imagine this alternative scenario: "Right team, this month I need you to sell twenty more cars, okay? That's twenty more cars than our usual monthly target because one of our key suppliers has increased their prices by almost forty percent. This means that the profit margin has dropped by forty percent, so that extra twenty cars is going to ensure that we keep on top of our profits. If we don't sell those extra cars, we wont be making as much money and as a result, we'll need to start removing some of the staff benefits and if we don't sell the extra cars, we'll need to let some of you go – do you think you can do it? That's it! Great! Let's remain motivated and focused, okay? Remember, you're a honey bear – now go claim your Hundred Acre Wood."

People need to understand why they are doing something in order to buy in to the task through a greater level of understanding. With that normally comes a deeper sense of emotional intelligence and connection with the task, too.

Try Again

If I told you what the current reoffending rate was in England you might be quite surprised. By reoffending rate, I mean the percentage of people who are convicted of a crime, serve a prison sentence and yet despite that punishment, then reoffend. At the time of writing, according the Government's own website, it is 58% and they reoffend in less than 12 months of being released from prison.

So, why do such a significant amount of people seemingly not learn their lesson? 58% would suggest that something isn't working. And it isn't. A revolution in the justice and punishment system is needed and it needs to involve psychologists and behaviourists to advise on the actually quite simple reason why so many reoffend. I'm not suggesting that this isn't a complex issue, which invariably is impacted by budget cuts, staffing issues and a plethora of other political issues, however, fundamentally, this is about people and changing their behaviour. What does the judicial system have to do with you? Well, the reason so many reoffend is because the feedback they receive for their crime, comes way too late - long-term consequences do not lock into association with behaviour as strongly as immediate consequences do. So if, for example, you were to break into a house, which I'm sure you wouldn't as I like to think that the readers I attract are of high moral standards, intelligent and fantastically attractive, too, but let's assume you did and you were caught. You'd be interviewed by the police and kept at a police station until they were ready to bail you, pending a court appearance. That could well be several weeks or months. Eventually you appear in court and are sentenced for burglary and sent to prison but your prison sentence could well start many weeks or months after the crime you committed. It's certainly not as immediate or with sufficient enough consequences compared to, say, burning yourself with an iron. And you probably know as well as I do that you have no intention of touching a hot iron again any time soon. Which is exactly my point. Feedback has to be immediate, whether that be a punishment or a reinforcer, to have the best long-term influence on our behaviour and that of others, too.

Carrot or Stick?

The choice of whether to change behaviour using a carrot (a positive reinforcer) or a stick (a positive punishment) is an old one and an argument I used to involve myself in regularly. I've heard every argument for and against both and to be frank, the discussion bores me now. As far as I'm concerned, if you're championing changing behaviour by force, fear or threats then I'm not interested in talking to you; at least not about that subject anyway. You're probably going to be the sort of person who believes in ridiculous conspiracy theories and enjoys arguing with people, too. My evidence-hungry, positively reinforced brain has little time for people who have opinions about things they know nothing about and who you hang around with matters so much that when people tell me about their tactics of intimidation and punishment to change behaviour, I tend to switch off, change the subject or have even been known to simply walk away. I know it's rude and if my Mum reads this she'll be terribly disappointed with me, but some things I have no energy left for anymore. Ignorance is one of those things. People who use these tactics to change behaviour are normally none the wiser; they know no other way and their response is "but it works." Concentration camps worked to wipe out millions of people but it wasn't the right thing to do: just because something works, it doesn't make it the correct, default response. I have all the patience in the world to teach people and to show them methods that are more efficacious or more effective, please don't misunderstand me, but I just don't have the desire to argue with people on the subject; you can't force people to change and more often than not a little bit of knowledge does a strange thing to a person - it gives them a feeling of almighty power as the old saying goes: you can lead a horse to water but you can't make him use a pencil.

So how then is it possible to get people to do what you want or need them to do? How can we nurture in ourselves and in others the possibility of getting extraordinary results? By changing how we approach changing behaviour. I'm not talking about brainwashing here. I appreciate that sometimes the idea of changing someone's behaviour can sound a little hypnotic and science fiction-esque. If you are at all interested in what brainwashing really is, I can highly recommend the fantastic book by Kathleen Taylor: *Brainwashing: The science of thought control*. I was interviewed alongside Kathleen for an episode of BBC Radio 4's popular show *All in the Mind*, hosted by psychiatrist Raj Persaud. We spent a good deal of time talking about her then new book and her research into the area of brainwashing; it's not at all how its portrayed in the films and is a part of our lives more than you might care to imagine. Anyway, that aside, here is my guide to getting people to do what you need them to:

Extraordinary Results from Ordinary People

In a somewhat ironic twist, getting extraordinary results is actually relatively simple. It just takes a little bit of consideration and to do the correct things...

1 Consider the importance of communication. In the medical field there is a maxim used for training: see one, do one, teach one. Essentially it covers the three key areas of learning styles: visual learning by watching someone do the task, manual learning by carrying out the task for yourself having just watched it being done, and finally embedding by teaching the skill to another person. This method of teaching - and learning - works so well for a multitude of reasons: not only is the individual encouraged to expose themselves to different learning styles, helping to ensure that their individual learning style is met but to experience others, which they may not normally opt for. However, it also allows the individual to discover for themselves how important it is to be clear in your instructions and to think about the task in different ways in order to effectively teach the task to someone else. I urge you to adopt this method of communicating wherever possible: show someone what you want them to do, have them do it and then teach someone else to do it, even if that someone else is you. You never know, you might learn something.

2 Always, always, always explain why the task needs to be done. When we don't understand why we are doing something, we are generally less compliant. With a greater understanding of the reasoning behind the task, we feel closer to it; can conceptualise the task better and can take ownership through fuller understanding.

3 Which brings me onto the next critical point: check their understanding of the task. Don't leave it until it's too late to find out that they either didn't understand or thought they understood but actually did something different to what you required. After explaining what you need to be done, have them report back their understanding of what they are going to do. This simple task often immediately raises issues in how they've interpreted your instructions and allows you the opportunity to see where they put importance on the instructions.

4 It's not me, it's you. It never fails to amuse me when people blame others for not carrying out what they were told when the only information they had to go on was what they were given. It almost always isn't the other persons fault – it's yours. You failed to communicate in a way that they understood, or didn't provide an environment whereby they felt confident enough to question your instructions, or you failed to check their understanding or failed to monitor their output. The sooner we start taking 100% responsibility for our decisions and choices and the consequences of those choices, the better we'll all be and the quicker we'll start getting extraordinary results. It's sometimes very difficult for people to comprehend that their own conscious understanding of something, cannot be grasped by someone else. It's like looking at an orange and the other person calling it a banana. But that's how it is for some people. Personally, I wish I met more people that saw bananas, where I saw oranges. That reminds me of an illegal rave I worked at once (I was there in a professional capacity!), where drugs and alcohol use was in abundance. One man wasn't overly enjoying his LSD-induced high because he'd begun hallucinating, seeing the other ravers as fruit. Where I saw a sweaty, wide-eyed, pale man gurning the life out of his jaw, he saw an apple. Where I saw a girl covered in beer, jumping around, swinging her hair to the incessant beat of the noise - sorry, music - he saw a pear. And this man took it upon himself to sort the other ravers (read pieces of fruit), into fruit bowls; grouping them into nice selections of oranges, bananas, pears, apples etc. I imagine when he's not off his face on acid, he's a very tidy man; very organised. Only, no-one else shared his hallucination and simply saw him as a man dragging them away from the friends they were with, to join a group of other bewildered people, equally high and undoubtedly experiencing their own hallucinations. As the fruit bowl task became more and more of a disaster, with bananas, apples and plums wandering off from their respective bowls and mixing with other fruits, the man became more and more distressed. It was one of the strangest things I've ever experienced.

5 The behaviour you want to see more of must be reinforced. Be patient though and reinforce any and all behaviours that are even a tiny bit in the direction towards the final behaviour you're looking for. Don't wait out to get the complete, perfect, finished product because often we need encouragement and recognition of our journey towards the end goal. If you taught basket weaving or pottery or even baking and waited before reinforcing anyone until they produced a perfect basket, a finished pot or a tasty pie, you'd be there, probably alone, for a long time.

6 The reinforcer must be reinforcing! Remember that what one person finds reinforcing, another won't. Discover what it is that the individual finds reinforcing; a verbal "excellent!," a hand written note, time out to call them, a bar of chocolate, recognition in front of their team?

7 Before they carry out the task, discover if there are any existing, or anticipated, barriers that may prevent the task, or their understanding of the task. When you've discovered them, work to remove them.

8 It's not all about the money. Remember that people want purpose, so empower them to achieve something more; be a part of something in which they can be proud and share their achievement with others. In turn, this becomes reinforcing and is a very powerful strategy. One of the simplest ways to achieve this is to offer responsibility for a part of the task or overall project, for example.

9 Don't forget to apply the +10% Principle. By setting realistic, achievable targets or goals, the achievement of which is in itself reinforcing the desired behaviour, we encourage people (including ourselves), to continue performing. The power of this is that the performance is often way over the 10% that they set out to achieve, so you all get more than you set out to get.

CHAPTER 5

EYE OPENING

"No act of kindness,
no matter how small,
is ever wasted."

Aesop, Revered ancient Greek storyteller.

Timely Reminders

I really love Aesop's Fables. Even when I was younger I did and I remember being read The Tortoise and The Hare as Mrs Wilson, my primary school teacher, pointed out the importance of the moral. But then, at fifteen, I found a copy in an antique book shop and gripped by nostalgia, flicked through. Only the bright, colourful cartoons were nowhere to be seen and the stories were dark. Really dark. Sinister even. Surely this was some sort of mistake? It was then, while stood in a dusty old antique shop in Henley; the pale, elderly owner of which watching me closely like a suspicious hawk and sweating like Marlon Brando after Thai food, that I began leafing through a copy of Aesop's Fables. These were the ones he really wrote, not the dumbed down, glitter-coated children's versions and it was here that my fascination with his stories really began. The metaphors and messages and inspiration I garner from his work has made a lifelong impression on me. I think the current copy of the Fables I own is my sixth one; they get read and referenced so often that the pages wear and the covers get tatty, so I regularly replace them. As I typed out the quotation to the start of this chapter, attributed to Aesop, I remembered an image I was sent on Facebook some time ago. It was titled "19 Signs You're Doing Better Than You Think." I don't remember who wrote it but it went something like this:

1. You are alive.
2. You are able to see the sunrise and the sunset.
3. You are able to hear birds sing and waves crash.
4. You can walk outside and feel the breeze through your hair and the sun's warmth on your skin.
5. You have tasted the sweetness of chocolate.
6. You didn't go to sleep hungry last night.
7. You woke this morning with a roof over your head.
8. You had a choice of what clothes to wear today.
9. You haven't feared for your life today.
10. You have overcome some sort of significant obstacle and as a result you have learned something and survived.
11. You often worry about what you're going to do with your life - your career, your family, the next step - which means you have ambition, passion, drive and the freedom to make your own decisions.

12. You live in a country that protects your basic human rights and civil liberties.

13. You are reasonably strong and healthy - if you became unwell today you could recover.

14. You have a friend or relative who misses you and looks forward to your next visit.

15. You have someone with whom to reminisce about 'the good old days'.

16. You have access to clean drinking water.

17. You have access to medical care.

18. You have access to the Internet.

19. You can read.

Whoever wrote it should be very proud; it is a list worth committing to memory and reminding ourselves of more regularly. Life is not just about being grateful for what we do have but is about being able to put our lives and what happens to us into perspective, too. The truth is that despite whatever is happening in your life, right now, you are probably not doing just a little bit, but a lot better than many other people in this world. We could do a lot worse than to remind ourselves of that more often, too. I think lists like this are worthy of being printed out and pinned above desks, or framed in hallways or pasted onto the sides of buses or billboards. They offer such strikingly simple, some may argue obvious advice, yet, the likes of which we just don't remind ourselves of often enough. When you feel yourself on the edge of a meltdown because your daughter has taken a felt tip pen excitedly to the wallpaper, reminding yourself that you woke up and were able to choose the clothes you are standing in and that you have not feared for your life today or had the opportunity to see the sun rise (you were, admitted probably still asleep), not only puts the challenges you are faced with into perspective, but makes it very difficult to selfishly continue down the path of a meltdown over what is essentially something arguably trivial and certainly repairable. You really should get up early one day and watch the sun rise. It changes something inside you. Perhaps as you are reading this, you might well think that it sounds like a good idea, but that you probably will not in fact do it. So why not set your alarm now? Set your alarm for super early so you get up to make a mug of something warming to help wake you up that you can sip and cradle in your hands as you watch life spring into action tomorrow morning.

While on the subject of Facebook, I just took a break from writing and replied to a message someone had sent me there. While I was logged on I saw that someone had posted a photo of a note, which they have printed out and stuck above their desk in their office. Occasionally people send me things like this, which makes having a Facebook account and being subjected to status updates about the mundane actions of complete strangers' cats, or public emotional outbursts just that little bit more tolerable. It is attributed to Robin Sharma and it reads:

The Rules For Being Amazing

Risk more than is required. Learn more than is normal. Be Strong. Show courage. Breathe. Excel. Love. Lead. Speak your truth. Live your values. Laugh. Cry. Innovate. Simplify. Adore mastery. Release mediocrity. Aim for genius. Stay humble. Be kinder than expected. Deliver more than is needed. Exude passion. Shatter your limits. Transcend your fears. Inspire others by your bigness. Dream big but start small. Act now. Don't stop. Change the world.

I wish I had written that. It is poetic and almost perfect. It is succinct and covers most of what being amazing would require, I think. However, the words amazing and extraordinary are often used interchangeably, at least colloquially, even though their actual definitions are actually quite different. Sometimes all we need is a simple reminder that we can be better; we can try harder; what we believe is as important as what we do and the simplest of things are often the most effective. It is interesting that two of those reminders have come recently via Facebook, which I try not to spend much time on. It saddens me to see young people near constantly staring down at their smartphones. I wonder if in a few years' time we will develop hunched backs or chronic neck problems because of the regular hyper flexion? Social media is one of those necessary evils in many ways for businesses such as mine, so I try to involve myself the minimum that I need to, for fear of turning myself into a social outcast. Mrs Jez has an addiction to Candy Crush, the modern day version of Tetris, only with fruit and the sooner she admits it, the better. I forget who it was but many, many years ago someone gave me the best piece of advice anyone ever has, on the subject of creativity. I was trying to design an interactive training session but was struggling to find anything that was sufficiently different or unique. Everywhere I looked I was faced with examples of things that plenty of other people were doing that were far from original and not sufficiently different to satisfy my creativity. The advice this person gave me was to look way back in time because people tend to chase the new and current things; they want to buy the newest technology or equipment; are drawn in by the latest book or DVD but somewhat ironically the older ideas that people have forgotten about have been neglected and unseen for so long that when used they in themselves become new. As an avid collector of antiquarian books, this was easy for me to put into place as I own an entire library of books on all manner of subjects, so I delved into books from as far back as the eighteenth century to discover inspiration long forgotten. Like much in life, fashions and designs are cyclical: as television viewers we are subjected to a wave of gardening programmes until they fall out of fashion, only for house renovation programming to take over before that falls out of favour and is replaced by magic and variety shows, shortly followed by comedy and sketch shows, then reality programmes like Big Brother and Gogglebox and before you know it, we are being educated again on the benefits of early, harsh pruning of buddleia and how to plant effectively for shady areas.

The subject of my recent talk at the TEDxMiltonKeynes conference was about our perceptions of generosity and greed and one of the themes I discussed was our seemingly innate desire to chase bigger, better and faster. In reality, we are chasing the positive effects felt from the dopamine release, as a result of getting the bigger, better or faster thing and not actually the things themselves. Dopamine is the chemical neurotransmitter released into our brain, which associates with happiness and reward. One of the points I raised in that talk was that if we understood why we do the things we do just a little better, we would know that when we buy another pair of shoes, it is not the shoes themselves that makes us happy; nor is it the expensive holiday or the big house in the country that we long for that makes us happy, it is in fact the dopamine (and a few other brain chemicals, too), that creates that feeling of happiness and fulfilment. However, happiness and fulfilment, the positive feeling we innately chase, can be found in other non-material things, too, which we can find closer to home; those things which we know matter most: our family, our friends and our pets, for example. If we sought our dopamine fix in things such as these instead, we would not only find ourselves much happier because we can access them more readily, more frequently and more cost effectively but we would also change our brain's neural network, to search in other areas for sources of happiness and fulfilment. Just how we improve our piano or guitar playing skills through repetition, or at least hope to improve them, changes to how we behave, can be achieved in much the same way. There is a saying, which is often attributed to Buddha, which states that "what we think, we become." The sentiment is especially relevant to how we can adapt our behaviour and actions and indeed choices and consequences if we adapt how we think. Interestingly, while doing research for this book, I discovered that there is no scriptural evidence that Buddha did ever in fact say that. It's yet another example of people not questioning their knowledge. According to the website Fake Buddha Quotes, the content of which is probably quite self-explanatory, 'what we think, we become' could possibly have developed from something that the Buddha did say, from the Dvedhavitakka sutta, in which he says: "Whatever a monk keeps pursuing with his thinking and pondering, that becomes the inclination of his awareness." Which isn't quite "what we think, we become."

Taking Stock

The reason for all this talk of Facebook and other worldly examples of what we read, like unrealistically perfect ideals, is to remind us to stop once in a while. To physically halt the fantastic pace at which we progress and continue through life and to take stock. When people ask me what my favourite activity is or what I enjoy doing at the weekend, I tell them I like to sit on a log, in a field and just look. I watch trees; grass; the sky; squirrels or any other wildlife or elements of nature that happens to be in my vision. Ants are especially nostalgic for me to watch as I'm sure you can now appreciate. Every time I see an ant going about its business, I am reminded of the choices I made and how nature undoubtedly played a huge part in saving my life. Very often people are surprised by the answer and I appreciate that the image of me, the person who runs across auditoriums leaping over the backs of chairs or dangling from chandeliers to help make presentations memorable, is sat in silence, doing nothing but looking, while at the edge of field, is quite a contrast. We can embrace these timely reminders, which surround us all, if only we take time to notice them and then appreciate them. The little things that make a big difference, surround us every day: the fact that you got up this morning. For the family whose mother or grandfather passed away in their sleep last night, your awakening this morning, something which you had absolutely no guarantee was going to happen and no biological control over, suddenly becomes more poignant. The smashed car window pales into insignificance when you realise that someone with a terminal illness would gladly swap it for your broken window. Seeing your child walk into the room is something the couple, whose child was stillborn, long for every second of every day. Even the fact that you can read this book, appreciate the vivid colours and mass of visual complexity the world, your garden and the cinema has to offer and see the faces of your friends and family is something that is worth taking stock of. According to Action for Blind People, around 360,000 people are registered blind or partially sighted in the United Kingdom (Access Economics, 2009) and nearly half of those people feel moderately or completely cut off from people and things around them (Pey, Nzegwu and Dooley, 2006). That alone makes me appreciate just my eyesight.

The process of stopping thinking, stopping the chase towards completing goals and achieving deadlines is extremely important for our own wellbeing; it provides opportunity for us to realise our own achievements and to pause in what often is a busy lifestyle, containing things which we have normalised to. A friend of my Mum's has recently moved into a large property, way out of their perceived budget. It's old with sweeping grounds and the previous owners agreed to leave all of the furniture with the sale of the house as it was their second country home and easier to let it go with the house. My Mum's friend was especially relieved because of the sheer size of the rooms; the furniture she had brought from her small three bedroom semi-detached house looked tiny and lost in the grand rooms! They negotiated a great price and live in what can only be described as a mansion; one of those right place, right time moments. In the extensive grounds of this house stands a Horse Chestnut tree, which her two sons thought was the best part of the whole move; their very own conker tree! I saw my Mum just yesterday and asked after her friend and the new house and she told me something in passing, which I want to share with you: my Mum's friends' two boys love conkers. They love exploring; they love being outdoors and the idea of playing conkers for them was the best thing about their new house! Just a few months after having moved in, the two boys no longer play conkers. Her friend told my Mum that the novelty of the conker tree had worn off. The boys had habituated to the abundance of conkers and now that little bit of magic has dwindled. What physical objects, people or resources are you surrounded by or have free access to, that you once longed for or worked hard to achieve? What elements of your life have you habituated to? One very real potential problem that will creep up on you unknowingly is that you create an ordinary life, or an ordinary view of what could well become an extraordinary life and all because you didn't take the time to take stock.

Crisis

As I type this, I'm sat in the beautiful Woodlands Park Hotel in Surrey. I have at this moment in time lost my memory stick, which has on it the only file which contains all of my book. It equates to about three months' worth of writing. To say I'm anxious would be a gross understatement; I'm bordering on depressed. Seriously. I normally warn people against diagnosing themselves with depression or low self-esteem and to first check that they are in fact not just surrounded by morons. However, I know that I really am feeling very low right now. Especially because in the three months prior to today, I have been working a lot on my book, every day, in order to get it finished for a deadline. There is a bitter irony in my lost memory stick. I usually back up all of my data but as I have been traveling so much recently, I have been working solely from that memory stick. There is no backup. I know, I can hear you tutting and rolling your eyes from here; I've learnt my lesson. So, being the optimist that I am, I feel that I should offer some advice to you, so that you can learn a lesson from my mistake. And here it is: do not buy a giant rubber tag to attach to your memory stick in the safe hope that you will not misplace or lose it. I am living proof that the theory and practice of this are both flawed. As at the time of writing, the entire book has been lost - along with the giant rubber tag attached to it. I'm going to press on and write, from memory, from where I left off in the hope that the distraction of writing numbs the pain I'm feeling at losing my book and that it turns up and I can simply slot this part in. If you're reading this and it's a page in a book, I either found the memory stick or found the will to re-write the whole thing. I guess you'll find out soon.

It Quickly Becomes Ordinary

In Sir Ken Robinson's excellent book Finding Your Element, he writes about the sheer amount of information that us humans are producing. As a species we seem to almost be obsessed with creating and distributing new information. For example, in 2010 the CEO of Google, Eric Schmidt, estimated that every two days we are producing as much information as we did from the dawn of civilisation up until 2003. Isn't that extraordinary? Thousands of years' worth of information every two days. Yet this mass production, this blizzard of data, is now ordinary for us. It's just what happens today in 2014: we design, create, write, upload, share and transfer information. It's a sobering thought that our extraordinary actions or characteristics may well be quite ordinary in no time at all, however, that shouldn't deter us from trying because it's highly likely that by the time your extraordinary is ordinary, you will in fact know nothing about it. You will be warmly cuddled up in a box surrounded by Mother Nature's very earth, or if you opt for it, scattered into particles; bits of you being eaten by fish, another bit of you fertilising daisies and yet more bits of you drifting about in the breeze, blowing into people's eyes.

The huge amount of information being created on a two-daily basis is testament to just what we can all achieve and enjoy being a part of. If we have an idea, why keep it to ourselves? Why not share it with everyone? Social media has certainly encouraged many of us to share our inspirations and creativity with instagram, our thoughts, our hopes and dreams on Facebook and our knowledge and opinions on twitter and Linkedin. Yet many of us don't have the courage to publicly produce or share the information we have within our minds. We don't like the idea that we might be wrong and that others will critically judge our thoughts or information, so we keep it to ourselves. Just imagine how much more information our species would produce if we all contributed the thoughts or ideas we had. Contrary to the popular phrase, there may not in fact be a book in all of us but that doesn't make our perspectives any less relevant and this is often where being extraordinary begins: taking an idea which you believe in and having the confidence to develop it, try it or implement it. Some things do not work but that doesn't make them any less relevant at the time. Many may not like the ideas you have, or agree with them but as the old adage goes: "you can't please all of the people all of the time." I personally don't believe in psychic ability and I do not agree with the practice of shamelessly preying on vulnerable people with promises of information that just teases, as poor and unvalidated evidence of the existence of spirits. However, despite my strong opinions on the psychic industry, it is worth an estimated one hundred million pounds a year in the UK, so my opinion on it clearly isn't having that much of an impact. If like me, you cannot be comforted by Tarot cards or Psychic Shirley, the likes of which I prefer to prefix with the word 'Allegedly', you should at least feel comfort in knowing that if your bursts of creativity, ideas or information aren't well received by some, there will be plenty of people who will embrace them. If something as vacuous as psychic ability can have so many followers then your idea for an inflatable dart board might not be as ridiculous as you first thought.

Euphoria

I was preparing to give my presentation this afternoon, doing the usual checks to make sure I had the pens I required, a glass of water and that the smoke machine and bin were in place when Fran, the co-ordinator from the events company organising the series of training events, came rushing into the room. She was on the phone and had a huge smile on her face.

Fran had been tasked on my behalf to contact the hotel where I thought my memory stick might be and plead with them to search the areas I'd been. Meanwhile, Mrs Jez had searched our house; my client, a manager of an automotive manufacturer, had searched my car along with a fellow presenter with their experience of taking cars apart (thankfully they put it back together) and I had been through the same pockets and luggage at least eleven times. Just in case. Fran had news that made me beam: the hotel had found my memory stick with the only backup copy of my book on it. What a huge relief. I must take this opportunity to thank Adam Briggs from Volkswagen, Steve Penson from Alisar, Fran Dodl from KTS Events and Eve Nichols, the receptionist from the Aztec West Hotel in Bristol, for playing their part in ensuring that this book actually was published because without them (and especially Eve and the kind person who handed my memory stick to reception), you wouldn't be reading this and I would probably still be slumped forwards, looking wistfully out of the window periodically wiping tears from my face. It's a shame the person who found my belt didn't have the same moral compass as the person who found the memory stick but the belt is replaceable. This book is itself now a little bit extraordinary, given the journey it has been on and the probability that it could have been lost forever! I've thrown the giant rubber tag away.

Starting

Of course you do not need a big vision or dream in order to be extraordinary or even create something that is extraordinary. Opting to do something out of the ordinary; something with a grander vision or greater impact does not in itself have to be worthy of an international prize. Your idea could be a simple one but may well have a big impact on how you work, think or behave or on how others work, think or play, or indeed to their life. The air ambulance network is an example of something that is essentially quite simple: loading a helicopter with, in the case of London's Air Ambulance, a specially trained paramedic and doctor with some equipment and flying them to those in need of life saving, critical medical intervention. Since 1989 when London's Air Ambulance was established and even then was one of the first helicopter emergency medical services, it has developed over time from that simple initial idea, to one which now includes first response cars for when the helicopter cannot fly; it was one of the first services to perform open heart surgery at the roadside and in the twenty five years it has been running, has helped save the lives of more than thirty thousand people. It is somewhat chilling to consider that whoever had that initial idea may not have shared it for fear of being ridiculed or because of the many challenges and barriers they would have faced, resulting in the death and disability of thousands more people. I have no doubt that there were many barriers that Dr. Alistair Wilson and his colleagues on the initial lobbying team at London's Air Ambulance would have faced, which at times may have seemed unsurmountable: clinical governance issues, initial financing, commitment to long term fundraising, development of specialist training, logistics, permission to land and local and national government approval being just some of them. It is worth noting that back in the late eighties, initially Tower Hamlets, the local council where the Royal London Hospital is based, refused to allow permission for the newly launched air ambulance to land on the landing pad atop the hospital. They believed the noise would be too loud for local residents. Not having permission to land is a serious problem for an airborne helicopter, made especially worse when you have an unwell patient on board and need to get them into a hospital. However, the belief in a thing is often all one needs in order to make it happen.

Faced with people who do not share your vision, perhaps through a lack of being able to clearly define what you envisage; red tape and obstructions from opposing parties can be far from encouraging. It can leave you feeling deflated and far from motivated to continue, however, in times like that I am always reminded and take comfort in the thousands of examples all around us of successful people. Success rarely comes easily. In fact, Thomas Edison is a perfect example of that. Not only did he rebuff the notion that he had failed to find a solution for his commercial incandescent lamp, as suggested by a reporter, but he publicly acknowledged that he had attempted thousands of times to find a solution. However, rather than viewing those attempts as failures, he positioned them as evidence that those particular methods didn't work, thus moving on to the next. Eventually of course he triumphed. Comedians and performers on television are often referred to as an "overnight success" when their premier television performance goes especially well. However, what many do not see are the ten, fifteen or more years of hard work that has gone into writing, developing and crafting a performance to be good enough to feature on television. We don't see the countless performances in dingy clubs and pubs and far less glamorous venues; nor do we see the many times which they failed to win much more than a polite clap from the audience, let alone a rapturous applause. In reality, far from an overnight success. I remember seeing a poster in the office of a small business once; it said: "sometimes having your own business is difficult - and sometimes it isn't." You could replace the words "your business" with absolutely anything in your life because some days we just don't have that get up and go we had yesterday or the day before and some days, as much as you want to be focused, you just aren't. Yet some days you are on top of your game - and that's life. I think it is very easy for most of us to occasionally lose track of that though. When you temporarily lose sight of the end goal or no longer have a clear direction in your mind of that inspiration and motivation that first spurred you to change or start a project, we turn our attention to other things or we become frustrated at the long list of items on our to-do-list that are still there, taunting you with their unchecked boxes and lack of completion.

Fire

You would be forgiven for thinking that my life was one constant roller coaster of drama and that a new BBC soap called 'Jezstenders' will feature daily moments from my life. You have no idea how lucky you are to be reading this book! Not only was it nearly lost for all time because of my carelessness and lack of backing up but it could have burnt, too. As I type I'm at the Radisson hotel in Manchester, having just woken up. Later today I will deliver a presentation to a group of forty managers from an automotive company. Only, today was not the leisurely start to the day that I like to enjoy when preparing for work. I've just been stood outside, in the rain, at half past eight in the morning, along with several hundred other hotel guests and staff (and Gandhi). Okay, it wasn't the real Gandhi but a man who had obviously been in the shower when the hotel fire alarm sounded for long enough for us all to take notice and realise that it was not in fact a test or fault. If my memory serves me correctly, his name was Tom and he seemed quite jovial about his rather exposed position. Other than utter embarrassment or embracing the situation with both hands - well, one hand otherwise he really would have been exposed - there were not many other emotions he could have gone for to be honest; everyone else was dressed and he was the only person with a towel around his waist and a towel draped around his torso in a swaddling-like fashion. It was novel enough for me to ask for a photo with him. I also took the opportunity to film one of my weekly videos for TBE-TV, my online video channel, so it turns out that hotel fire alarms can in fact be quite useful.

Jez Rose and Tom Bryson wishing he'd kept a pair of jeans closer to hand.
[2014]

If you'd like the see the video and what I look like without my hair done or moustache primed, it's here: http://bit.ly/gandhirain

My client and colleague who were also presenting at the same training event were staying at the same hotel, so they got to see me without my moustache primed or my hair done and agreed that I looked like a psychopath. I am a walking, talking social psychology experiment you see: the responses to my moustache and beard are quite interesting. During the month of November when many men grow their moustaches out for the global charity event Movember, in aid of prostate cancer, I become part of a special and elite club. Women smile coyly as they pass me in the street and men tip their heads, winking approvingly. For an entire month I enjoy feeling like we are part of one big happy family with a common purpose. That is until the first of December when all the other men shave their moustaches off, having complained about the itching and that they looked like Tom Sellers for a month. Overnight, the approving looks and supportive comments that I enjoyed, turn into looks of disgust and distain, with women scrunching their noses up at me and men looking in desperation, as I instantly go from fellow club member, to pervert.

If the hotel had really been on fire, the additional ten thousand words I had written on my laptop, since finding my memory stick and having it sent to my house while I continued working away, would have been melted and lost forever, too. This book is doomed. If you are at all superstitious you should probably stop reading it now, or at least don't look at it before you fly. Stood outside in the rain, surrounded by hundreds of hotel guests at varying stages of being awake, did put something quite extraordinary into perspective, however. When I joined my colleagues, I looked around and saw plenty of people stood in silence; some staring at the floor, others on their phones and a fair few looking very angry, glancing at the hotel building with disdain. I very much doubt the hotel staff had secretly met the night before while we were all tucked up in bed to plot a spoof fire evacuation and the building itself couldn't help being on fire but nonetheless, there were angry looking people. I did what I always do when I have spare time on my hands: do something with it. I very much live my life for trying to learn, do, think, experience, embrace or otherwise fill every second of my life with an activity to make the very most of my time while I am here. To do otherwise seems a real waste of both time and of the many wonderful experiences there are for us to engage with; there's absolutely no chance of me slowing down or to stop taking on five projects at once because I have so much to fit into the finite time that I'm here. So, unable to do any work, I set about having my photo taken with Gandhi and making a video. Where possible, I try to make the weekly videos quite light hearted but with a message you can take away if you are in the mood to do so. I am a gregarious, positive person, which I do understand may be annoying for some but I really don't care much. So I took my phone out of my pocket and shot a quick video about the hotel fire alarm and how it reminded me just how resilient we can be as human beings; when we are faced with challenges or obstacles or things that don't quite go according to how you planned, we can find a positive in the situation, or learn a lesson. The fact that I did not have the opportunity to do anything with my hair, nor my moustache, coupled with the fact I was outside in the rain making a video about the evacuation, surrounded by hotel guests, seemed to pique the interest of a lot of guests. If you watch the video you can see many of them smiling, laughing and enjoying watching on at the, granted, slightly unusual response to a hotel fire alarm. And that is when it really came home to me just how simple doing something extraordinary can be. After I had made the video and we were allowed back into the hotel, many of those who were looking on at the video being made commented on how it brightened up their morning. I think the difference between a lot of ordinary things and extraordinary things is often simply that someone saw an opportunity to do something different, unexpected - or just to do something rather than nothing.

CHAPTER 6

THE PURPLE BANANA PRINCIPLES

"All men dream: but not equally. Those who dream by night in the dusty recesses of their minds wake in the day to find that it was vanity: but the dreamers of the day are dangerous men, for they may act their dream with open eyes, to make it possible."

T. E. Lawrence, prolific writer, celebrated British Army officer and Lawrence of Arabia.

The Purple Banana Principles

When you write a book called *Be a Purple Banana*, it prompts people to ask a lot of questions. Understandably. Principally, "what's it about?" and "what is a purple banana?" Which tucks neatly alongside "why don't we see much of you anymore?" and "you look tired." So I've compiled this list of principles, which may, or may not, help by offering you a starting point on your journey from ordinary to extraordinary. They are by no means definitive, exhaustive or prescriptive but I did feel that introducing the notion of how to take ordinary people and make them extraordinary and then simply talking around the subject wouldn't be especially helpful for a lot of people. So use these principles in their entirety if you wish, or use them to develop your own set of principles, guidelines and adjustments to your moral compass or understanding of what you, or the people you are in charge of, are in fact capable of. Equally, feel free to dismiss them all and make up your own; the process is an interesting and enlightening one and isn't so much about following set guidelines or principles but about questioning, pushing your own subconsciously determined boundaries and challenging those things which you accepted to be resolute, probably without even thinking about why.

Populate your life with people that matter to you and with those who will make a positive difference to your life as a result of being around them. I am reminded, by a magnet which sits on our fridge (even though no one in our house knows whose it is or how it got there), of the old adage: "you can choose your friends but you can't choose your family." While you may not be able to choose your family, you can choose how much time you spend around them and what to talk about, to protect how they make you feel. Some of the greatest impacts on our lives come from those we spend the most time around and allowing them to influence our decisions and behaviour.

Understand precisely what you want to achieve and plan for it. The clear goal you set yourself provides you with focus and clarity. Planning what you want is just the beginning; it is understanding how to do that, which is just like creating a map; it shows you the journey you need to take; the tasks to undertake and in which order. Without this clarity we open ourselves to procrastination and distraction and if we ever do get to our goal, it's likely to be a lot longer journey getting there than if we maintained focus.

Reflect on the progress you make. At the end of every week, take a couple of minutes to reflect on your week and note at least five positive things that happened. All too often we reflect on only the negative things and it can quickly seem everything bad happens at once as all of the negative things start to get on top of us, affecting our behaviour. In reality, of course, that's rarely the case, it's simply that we've been emotionally and psychologically placed to manage our time and the other things that haven't gone according to plan but there have also been plenty of good things to distract us and make us feel positive. In those moments when it appears "everything is going wrong," it's normally the case that we're tired or distracted or haven't taken the time to reflect on our achievements and the positive things; as a result, the negative things take centre stage and it appears to our battle-weary mind that everything is going wrong. People who achieve extraordinary things seem to keep a mental tally of every single step closer they are to what they want to achieve. The negative things, the mistakes and moments drifting off course don't get any free head space; they are sieved for anything worthy to add to the experience bank and then cast aside. The only things worth holding onto are milestones achieved.

Perspective is essential. Maintaining sight of your vision, dream, aspirations or reason for wanting to be different, achieve more or however you wish to develop higher performance, is critical. It's balanced perspective which allows us to not let the negative comments affect us and which helps us to make the correct decisions at the time, affecting the most appropriate consequences. Having perspective doesn't come easy to some people - and lots of those people seem to drive cars. It's the 'smashing a glass scenario': one thing that always helps me to maintain perspective is to ask: "did anyone die?" Nothing gets worse than the loss of life, does it? So if that didn't happen, it's better than the worst case scenario, so already things are looking up. Choose positivity.

Learn from your mistakes. It's easy to get caught up in life because the bills need paying, the washing needs to be done, clothes need ironing, we need to eat and then there's the cleaning and the gardening and the dogs that need feeding and walking and of course work; you have work to do - you get the idea. The behaviours we reinforce, we see more of but often there isn't anyone there to reward your efforts, so it's down to us. It's okay to take time to reflect on the positives; on the things you've done well and the moments you enjoyed. And while, generally, we are relatively good at doing that as we're searching for the next thing; the bigger house, the faster car, the more expensive clothes or the tastier pie, we are not especially good at taking time to objectively reflect on the things that didn't go so well. Objectively is the key word there. Firstly we tend to deny that it was our fault that something didn't go according to plan, or at the very least we offer a whole package of justifications to comfort us. It is important to bask in the glory of those things which go well but it is equally important to look candidly at those times where we make the wrong choice, or where we don't live up to our own expectations or established morals. It will inevitably be painful but from mistakes we learn. Mistakes offer us golden opportunities to tweak and improve for the next time because if we continue to do the same things, we will only get the same results; to get different results requires us to adopt different behaviours.

Everyone has a story. We've all got reasons to be grumpy or antisocial, which are justifiable to ourselves at the time because most of us live in the moment, with little or sometimes no regard for the future or even what has been. Being mindful of why someone may respond differently to the way in which you would and being patient of those moments of misjudged responses and behaviours, can prevent so much antagonisation. It is often this antagonising that elevates stress levels and breeds contempt, which are absolutely not conducive with higher performance.

Be clear about what it is that you want to achieve. Set out first with a clear goal and vision so that you remain focused on the end result. This will be invaluable when you are faced with challenges and moments of adversity. Remember that millions before you have been in the same position and in many cases, seemingly against all odds, have succeeded.

Always remind yourself of the difference that your journey to extraordinary will make to yourself and/or to others. We generally get much poorer levels of compliance from people when they do not understand why they are doing something, so being clear about why you want to be or do something extraordinary is equally important. This will help to convince others, as they in turn understand why you are doing it.

Never. Give. Up. Start by knowing that doing anything extraordinary is never as straightforward or as easy as you'd like it to be. There will be people who disagree with you and will make it their sole life purpose to challenge you or prevent you from doing anything other than ordinary things. Plenty of people will be there to discourage you and tell you that you can't, shouldn't or won't achieve. These people are ordinary and as much as you may love them or care about them, you cannot let their negativity stop your journey.

Annotate your life. One of the commonalities among those who have achieved extraordinary things, is that they have taken opportunity, where possible, to reflect and consider their achievements; the possibilities available to them and opportunities to make the next step from ordinary to extraordinary. I find that the best way to annotate your own life is through "blue sky thinking."

The term "blue sky thinking" refers to a creative process which is not limited, impacted or affected by your current knowledge or restrictions. I have no idea where the term originated or why it is called "blue sky thinking" and not, for example, "starry sky" thinking, which, for me, seems much more encouraging and limitless than a blue sky. However, the point is really that during the creative process, you should allow your mind to think freely and with no restriction. For example, you might be tasked with improving levels of customer service in the organisation you work for and you could suggest that every customer receives an all-expenses paid trip to Hawaii as a thank you gift for being a customer. That is blue sky thinking in action. Far from being fanciful or unrealistic, it helps to free your mind to think at its most creative. Only when all of your ideas are exhausted do you then begin to look more practically at the ideas you have listed. In the example I've given you would, probably, reason that sending every customer to Hawaii was not financially viable and look to make the same notion more affordable and practical, ending up with hand writing every new customer a thank you card and posting it to their home address. Would you have still got to that idea had you not originally gone through the blue sky thinking process? Well, that is debatable but like all the best ideas, they are often not only strikingly simple but the product of a creative process, influenced by many other factors.

You can do your own "blue sky thinking" exercise in a diary or journal or even on large pieces of paper, which is my personal preference. Or a whiteboard. Or you can do it on a piece of scrap paper. In fact anywhere really; it's a very flexible exercise. The concept of "blue sky thinking" is especially useful here as it allows you to not only reflect on how you have come to be doing what you are doing right now and in the way in which you are doing it, but also to consider how you could adapt or change, to alter the future. To be clear, when I say "annotate your life" I don't mean that you should write a diary; I certainly don't have the time nor inclination to write a diary. Instead, this "blue sky thinking" exercise will allow you creative freedom to do something that very few of us have done, certainly regularly, and that is to stop and take time to reflect on what opportunities you have missed; which choices you made which were perhaps not the best that you could have made and possibly more importantly, what you can do to change about where you are now.

No means no now - not forever. We aren't especially good at handling rejection as a species. I clearly remember the trauma of my first girlfriend ending our relationship, rejecting me for some jumped up ponce in a Porsche (which had a taped up broken back window). With hindsight I'm very pleased about it all but at the time, of course, it was incredibly painful and as someone who was regularly "dumped" (with terminology like that it's no wonder so many people are affected by it), you would think that I'd have habituated to the experience. But no.

Aside from personal childhood traumas, I have ten years' experience teaching leadership and sales teams worldwide and one of the common challenges faced by many of them is the fear of rejection: that the customer will say "no." As a result they either don't attempt to sell a particular product that they know runs a greater risk of being let down or they procrastinate to the point that productivity quite literally plummets. They become experts at doing the small things to make themselves busy, but neglect the very things that will secure their positions: selling.

Another day there will be a different story to tell and your life will be one more day further on, so whatever happens today is just happening today. Now, of course, there may well be spillage and events might flow over to another day or week - or even month. But nothing stands still - today's news is tomorrow's history, when tomorrow comes. Every second of our lives that ticks away becomes another minute that passes us by. Every hour that escapes us is another day that disappears and every Christmas that "came around so quickly" is full of both potential memories and opportunities for us to create extraordinary moments.

So there you have it; the principles on which I set out to define how ordinary people can achieve extraordinary things. It's largely introspective. Something which has had the greatest impact in my life, other than actively choosing to be positive, is changing the way that I respond to questions. In order for us to look at things differently, we must change the way that we respond to what is asked of us. For example, if I call a restaurant asking for a table at 7pm, I could be told: "No, because we are fully booked." If that was the case, I'm likely to hang up and call another restaurant – they would have lost a sale and I'd be continuing my journey to finding a restaurant that could accommodate me. Alternatively, I could be told: "Yes, if you come at 7.15pm." The difference will naturally have a commercial impact on the restaurant and those commercially savvy readers can feel free to forward cheques for the increased revenues your businesses make as a result of implementing this simple yet profound shift in psychology. Please make them payable to my adopted charity partner, the Contented Dementia Trust. However, it runs much, much deeper than that. We can all provide myriad excuses as to why things cannot be done. I don't know how or why that skill developed in humanity but it did. Perhaps there's some sort of developmental blip that will require us all to offer expertly crafted excuses as to why things cannot be done. On second thoughts, perhaps it's just a "politician gene" that we all carry, which gives us the ability to wiggle out of any situation. Try this: the next time you are asked a question, instead of responding with "no, because," respond with "yes, if" and in place of excuses for why it cannot happen, offer suggestions of how it could happen. This is normal practice in my office; in fact I sit underneath a huge sign which says: "No, because" which is crossed out and underneath is written: "Yes, if," as a constant reminder to everyone. This one change in positioning is the foundation of the behaviours that create my business. Language is so critical to the way that we think and subsequently how we behave that there are many books written entirely on that one subject. I present a two hour lecture on the word "can't" and its limiting repercussions on our behaviour. It's an especially damaging word to use around children. The language that we use, whether it is as part of our internal dialogue or when communicating with others, frames so much of how we think, what we think, why we think it and in turn how we behave or respond to the behaviour of others that its power cannot be underestimated. Research has shown that, for example, negative phraseology can prevent us from achieving the very thing we set out to achieve and conversely, positive language can assist us in achieving it quicker. Try it for yourself. It takes a little getting used to, as the automatic reaction is to offer reasons why something cannot be done, but stop yourself and start the response with: "Yes, if."

Can I ask you a question? If I may? It seems a bit strange, approaching you directly like this. Is it okay for an author to talk directly to a reader? I imagine there's a rule, like actors talking to an audience. Don't worry, I'm not going to ask to borrow money. If I were to ask you if you had any problems right now, either at home or work, how would you answer? Perhaps you don't have any problems now but that you recognise that you've had some in the past. I think almost everyone would agree with that. However, you can very simply get rid of all problems in your life and it's incredibly easy. I'll let you in on the secret: stop using the word problems. Simple.

Okay, so by not using the word problems, it won't actually get rid of the problems themselves. I appreciate that is perhaps a step too far. However, it does change how you perceive and respond to those so-called problems. Instead of using the word problems, consider using instead challenges or barriers. Those two words aren't so negatively charged as the word problem is, which has an almost abrupt connotation to it and they instead offer us a greater freedom in how we perceive the challenge or barrier: far from sounding negative they, at least to me, sound almost enticing, intriguing and inviting, as though they are teasing a possible solution. And it's that perception, which is key: do you perceive a challenge or barrier as something to find a solution to and work around? Or does it mark a definitive end? When I was studying behaviour, my professor made it clear that if we approached him with only problems, he would send us away with the same problem. "However," he would whisper in his gentle tone, which had a magical quality of intense wisdom to it, "if you come to me with a problem and a possible solution, I'll buy you a coffee and we can talk about it." Despite the fact that I don't drink coffee, I've adopted that same approach to any challenge or barrier I come up against: you find a solution, even if it's to at first simply navigate the presenting challenge, in order to get you back on course to your original goal.

JFDI (Just Flippin' Do It)

The Purple Banana Principles work. I know that because not only do I use them every day but so do thousands of others all around the world who I've presented them to or lectured to over the past ten years. However, reading this book could be a fantastic waste of your time and a waste of the money you paid for it, too - unless of course it was a disappointing gift - if you do nothing with the principles. Passive reading is for novels, comics and newspapers, but is not for books like this. If you read passively, you don't absorb the information and that would be a real shame. If you were given this book and it's turned out to be a disappointing gift, you could give it to a least favourite child or use each individual page to decorate a wall in your office or house, lightly covered with wallpaper paste to seal them. I saw that in a shop once and always thought it would make a really unusual wallpaper effect. So in that respect, it's not an entirely disappointing gift, is it?

What I'm most interested in is what makes us do the things we do. Why is it that some people seem brilliant at their job? Can that energy and apparent magnetism be learnt? How is it that some people's ability and behaviour can be so intrinsically different to that of our own - or of others? Is there a special something that makes people do extraordinary things, or gives them the ability to be better at something than they are currently? And the answer is a resounding "yes." Which is just as well, otherwise this book would not only have been incredibly short, but fantastically unfulfilling, too. Much like those tiny chocolate eggs that turn out to be hollow. Chocolatiers can be a cruel, cruel group.

All of our behaviour produces consequences. And of course those consequences can be good or bad, however, before the behaviour happens, there is something called an antecedent. This is the thing that occurs before the behaviour happens, that triggers the behaviour. For example, you might punch someone and as a consequence they get a bloody nose and you, quite rightly, end up in the comfortable surroundings of a police car. Before you punched them though, something happened to cause you to do that. Perhaps you were at Disneyland and an irritatingly chipper employee told you one too many times to "have a nice day." The kids were screaming, you were all tired and something just snapped in you. It's understandable - although not excusable, so remember that the next time you're holidaying in Florida. Perhaps you started eating a lot of high fat content foods and as a consequence, you put on a lot of weight. However, before you started eating burgers, chocolate and ice cream, your beloved hamster, Hammy, died and left a seemingly irreparable empty hole in your life. Until about three months later when you'll buy another one. So, the antecedent comes before the behaviour. For many people who have no knowledge of learning theory or behaviour, this is a revelation that behaviour is a three step process, not a two-step one.

The chain of an Antecedent, which prompts a Behaviour, which in turn results in a Consequence is often referred to as the ABC of behaviour for, I hope, obvious reasons. In many cases, understanding our behaviour, its likely cause and its subsequent control, is as simple as A, B and C. Although that does not necessarily mean that it is easy, as that is very often not the case. This insight into behavioural psychology will prove to be especially useful I'm sure. If I was to ever write an instructional manual for humans; the one we didn't get when we were born, I think I'd begin by explaining just how our behaviours come about and how they are encouraged or suppressed. It is the one thing I talk about when presenting or lecturing, which so many people tell me was especially useful. I suppose it's because it is so simple yet so enlightening and offers an explanation to so many behaviours, of our own and of others, that may not have been understandable or explainable before. In those three letters: A, B, C, we get an insight into why our dog pulls like a steam train when heading towards the park (the consequence to his pulling is that you continue walking closer to the park, therefore, reinforcing him with the greatest doggy reward of all: play at the park and before the pulling behaviour, you put the lead on and let him pull in the first place); why a particular child in class may demonstrate challenging behaviour (there are myriad explanations but understanding that the focus shouldn't be on the behaviour itself but on its cause encourages us to approach the situation differently) or why some days we are irritable and argumentative (perhaps we didn't go to bed early enough the night before and we are running on insufficient sleep). Simple? In essence, yes. Certainly simple enough to take a moment to consider your own behaviour and that of others, which particularly stands out, and then to reflect what the antecedent may have been. Behaviour doesn't just happen.

Gone

Writing about the consequences of our behaviour comes at an especially poignant time. I woke up this morning, as I do most mornings - thankfully - and reached for my phone. I'm a real 'morning person' and at my most creative and active first thing. The earlier the better, too. However, despite this, or in spite of this, the act of getting up is quite often a difficult one for me. It's the removing of my comfortable body from the warm, cosy bed-pit that I struggle most with. Once I'm up, it's absolutely fine but I need something as soon as I wake up to engage my brain and stimulate my neurons. This is the only time I read the news. I generally cannot stand reading newspapers as they've been full of so many untruths and misguided articles written about people I know, that I've come to actively distrust their content. The free one we have delivered on a Saturday is extremely useful to get the fire started in the winter though, so I'm not entirely ungrateful for their existence. So, I wake up and reach immediately for my phone, which sits on my bedside cabinet and proceed to check the news headlines. I don't tend to read the articles for reasons already cited but the concentration on the headlines and processing the various consequences does help to waken me. Today was no different, only today I woke up Mrs Jez when I said, quite loudly, "Oh, please no!" Robin Williams, one of my greatest comedy inspirations, has died.

I found it quite hard to concentrate all morning, so I went for a walk with my dogs; something which forces time to myself and allows me some quiet reflection. As I was walking through the fields, I felt a strange sense of being slightly removed. Removed from the world which my dogs were enjoying; running around chasing each other, darting in and out of the river, splashing and having fun. Removed from society a bit, I guess. I felt removed from fun – from life. As I walked through the beautiful Northamptonshire countryside in England, which I'm so fortunate enough to live in, the sun slowly fading behind the trees, the fields a beautiful lush green and the trees a myriad of different colours of green. The stillness was palpable. There is a natural beauty to my surroundings, in every sense of the word, and the isolation from the rush of everyday life; from people and machines, is both refreshing and enrapturing. One of my favourite times to walk is when a gentle breeze rustles the leaves of the trees, as it did on this walk. But I'm feeling removed as I think of Williams and his tragic death. Tragic for him and for his family, of course, but for me and millions of others around the world, too. In itself that feeling of being removed from that moment in which my dogs were enjoying so intently, as I looked on, and feeling removed from everyone else's lives; indeed from life, is an insight into what it's like to experience depression. As I reflected on that, I began thinking of the many quotations in life, which are shared and repeated so often and which have spurred an entire cottage industry of t-shirt, mug and mouse mat printing: "Happiness is a state of mind; it's just according to the way you look at things" (Walt Disney); "No matter what people tell you, words and ideas can change the world" (Robin Williams) and "You'll have bad times, but it'll always wake you up to the good times you weren't paying attention to" (Williams again). These quotations, captured during interviews and poignant parts of film performances inspire us; they spark an interest in us and lift us up but for a moment. However, these reflections shouldn't only be momentary. Their meaning is far more powerful than simply throw away quips. They have the power to affect people; to change the way in which we work, the way that we interact with people and how we model ourselves. These quotations and sage pieces of advice can change the way we behave. These comments, which are shared around social media, used to decorate office walls and punctuate presentations, deserve greater consideration. How can we apply this advice practically, to shape our behaviour in the long-term and therefore, the consequences of our behaviour?

As I stood in the fields with my dogs, looking at the vast expanse of countryside, not a single person or indeed human intervention in sight, the beauty was staggering. The bright blue, azure sky; the gentle breeze and the enchanting stillness. The lack of people and the opportunity my surroundings provide for reflection, creates an almost magical quality. Yet I couldn't help but feel that some of this is indeed what caused some of Williams' pain, which led him to take his own life: this isolation that I enjoy is the very factor which causes such distress and sometimes results in someone taking their life. I know because I've been there. I understand that this loneliness and isolation can manifest with overpowering realism, regardless of the actual immersion in love, care and affection. Everything in life can be seen in different ways, from different perspectives. And so Walt Disney was wrong. It's not just happiness but indeed everything in life. It is all according to the way that we choose to look at it. There are many entertainers such as Stephen Fry, Ruby Wax, Catherine Zeta-Jones and Richard Pryor who, like Williams, have publicly shared their mental health challenges. For all of the heartache and the seemingly impenetrable struggle, which depression enforces, I for one, cannot help but have an almighty respect for its gravitas. It would appear that some of our most creative entertainers, whose gift to make us laugh and suspend our disbelief to escape reality but for a moment, suffer from mental health issues. Yet without them, they would not be the same people. The depression, the bi-polar, the alcoholism, and the drug addictions – these are parts of their intricate and delicate tapestries. Even if they were as creative and funny and loved without the alcohol and the depression, would they believe the affection? Would they see what we admire in them? Is the manic, frenetic creativity, which creates such unique products of entertainment, actually a necessary evil? One thing is for sure, it is the very thing that makes them and often, the very thing that breaks them, too. Without his neurological makeup, Williams wouldn't have been the Robin Williams we knew. The Robin Williams we loved. The Robin Williams I miss so much. Now although this book is not about mental illness, it is about behaviour and given that depression and other mental health issues, which covers moments of feeling blue and a bit down, affects 1 in 4 of us here in the UK, I believe that we need to embrace a greater understanding of mental illness. The fragility. The power. The unnerving presence shouldn't be something which we no longer talk about. If you're feeling "a bit depressed" or "sad" or entertaining "the black dog," as Sir Winston Churchill referred to his bouts of depression, or however you wish to describe it, it doesn't make you crazy. It does, however, make you human. Whether you have or you haven't yet experienced some form of mental health issue, I believe that making a choice as to how you let your behaviour impact you and those around you, can help not only develop a higher performance, but to manage our mood, too. I feel I do need to be clear here that this does not belittle any genetic or diagnosed mental health issues. I'm not saying that simply changing the way you think will cure you. I am saying that it's much more powerful than you think and along with the many efficacious drugs and therapies around, could be a strategy that will help. If you don't have a mental health issue, it's still relevant because if you react to something in such a way that is irrational, or behave in a manner that is over the top or even make a misjudged decision, *Be a Purple Banana* was written for you, too. The death of Robin Williams has shown us that it is time for all of us to look inward and reach outward, to start changing the way that we behave and to not just talk about it. Action will in turn change not only our own behaviour but that of others around us, too. It's time to start looking a little more seriously at the laughter.

Perception

The way we perceive something and the opinions we allow ourselves to have on any given matter are flexible. If you are reading this book I am assuming you have a degree of power over yourself: no one has a gun to your head forcing you to have opinions about things you know little about. Having bared witness to some ridiculous, cruel, thoughtless and misguided and downright stupid actions - as you will have, too - I admit to sometimes struggling with the stupidity of humans. The British comedian John Cleese tells a story about when he was teaching in a school and a colleague with an especially dry sense of humour said: "You know, John, the very sad thing about real stupidity is that there is absolutely nothing you can do about it." However, while others may give up on people, I see within each person I meet, potential. We all can strive to be better people and for better results in what we do and it is my opinion that we should, too. We change, or adapt, readily, when we seek knowledge and ask questions. I don't necessarily mean by actively learning or seeking to study in an academic sense but the act of questioning our own knowledge, our morals and beliefs is key to growing and developing as a person and to achieving extraordinary feats. I don't know who said it, but I remember being at a conference where someone quoted the phrase: if you do what you've always done, you'll get what you've always got. In other words, if we don't change, you cannot expect to achieve anything differently and, as I'll explore a little later, getting something different to what you've always got, begins inside your own mind and with the language that we use. So I'd encourage you to not take other people's opinions and simply make them your own. We must form our own opinions, based on fact, accurate judgement and knowledge and if we don't have those things to hand we must take more comfort in knowing that it is okay to not have an opinion about something. Now, please don't think me fantastically prescriptive and anti-opinions because I'm not. I'm aware that I'm beginning to sound like a middle class toff like you'd get in a pub, raising their opinionated voice loud enough so that other people outside of their own party can hear them. I've never even owned a Volvo and there was just the once when I draped my jumper around my shoulders but it was for purely practical reasons. However, my journey to understand what it is that makes ordinary people able to do extraordinary things has shown me this: that there is a commonality in those people who think or achieve extraordinary things and that is the ability to think independently; to nurture intrigue and to seek out more knowledge to test their existing knowledge. It's a knowledge Top Trumps of sorts. Having discussed this desire with now so many people I have interviewed, it seems to be about developing greater confidence in the knowledge and opinions they have. Having an opinion about something is important and we live in a free society where we have the ability to do so, which should be embraced and respected but by seeking to actively check our opinions, we can be surer of the statements we make, which makes stepping out of our knowledge comfort zones easier to do because while the results may not be known, the hunch or opinion we have is not simply plucked from thin air but born from our collective knowledge and experiences and the challenging of those things. As American author Eudora Welty said: "Don't be like the rest of them, darling."

Comfort Zones

"Do you know there are people who choose to die in a burning building rather than run outside with their pants off?" the social psychologist Stanley Milgram writes. Presumably he wasn't the one giving them that choice in some bizarre (and frankly cruel) psychology experiment. Living within a psychological and behavioural comfort zone is, by definition, comfortable. From where our mugs are kept in the kitchen, to our favourite mug for tea and the length of time we leave the tea to brew and then how much milk we add, all the way through to the route you take to work and what you wear to work are ingrained behaviours that form our comfort zones. I once met someone who confided that he not only had socks with days of the week printed on them but also had pants, which he'd had his wife sew little labels with the days of the week on. If that wasn't slightly odd in itself, he told me that he felt out of sorts if he wasn't wearing corresponding socks and pants to that particular day. Grab a pencil and mark that piece of the book to re-read when you think you've got problems. Anyway, comfort zones are so named because the behavioural and psychological area that we naturally like to be in is anxiety-neutral. That is, comfortable and one we can be at peace with. Not at all like the state you find yourself in when your friend's annoying partner comes round. All of the behaviours that define our comfort zone are boundaries of sorts that we develop over time; things that we decide we are, or are not, comfortable with - that either make us slightly anxious or keep us free from anxiety and which, in turn make us feel safe and secure. Doing something out of the ordinary or experimenting with different behaviours and alternative ways of doing things takes us outside of our comfort zones. And that is something many people find very difficult to do indeed.

Security is a key, innate need of us humans. People who live on the Isle of Man seem to have lived the longest of any Western society I know with so much trust and an innate feeling of security. I was on the island for the first time several years ago, presenting to a financial group and as the taxi driver took me from the airport to the hotel, he gave me a verbal historical tour of "Mann." He'd lived on Mann all of his life and told me that up until recently, no one locked their front doors. They all knew each other and so tight knit and close was the community on the island that no one bothered. He told me how his neighbour moved away off of the island and a new family moved into the house, only to be woken the next morning at just gone seven in the morning by banging in the kitchen. Fearing an intruder, the husband made his way downstairs brandishing a slipper, presumably to attack the intruder with an additional level of comfort, only to find the island's postman in their kitchen making a cup of tea for himself, having duly laid out the family's post on the kitchen table. Both men were as shocked as each other at the unexpected sights. The taxi driver went on to say how times were changing and that more people were locking their front doors on Mann now, although I was reassured it was not because of the postman.

Actively doing something, whether that be a new behaviour or changing an existing behaviour, that changes the set boundaries of our comfort zones, doesn't come easy for most and understandably so. It's more than about being 'set in our ways' and nothing to do with being stubborn. We seem to be aware, all-be-it for many subconsciously, of the fragility and complexity of life. To help combat the uncertainty and feelings of anxiety and self-consciousness we experience when we are without patterns of familiarity, we have taken to driving the same routes to work, reading books by the same authors, visiting the same websites, cooking the same core meals and having things 'just so' in our homes. Given this, it's little wonder why so many people struggle to understand just how they can be anything more, or different than how they are right now when they are seeking and surrounding themselves with the same information and repeating similar behaviours. To achieve different results it can simply be a case of doing the same thing but differently: choosing a different route to work to engage your mind or inspire you; reading other authors and seeking information from alternative sources. I'm a real education geek: I love learning. That's one of the reasons that my library has amounted to over 3,000 books; I just can't stop reading and learning. However, my inner geek isn't satisfied with simply reading at my own leisure; I have an addiction to courses, too. I'm currently half way through another degree; an open degree with the Open University this time, which allows me to essentially select a variety of subjects and modules to study. It's not quite as diverse as studying nineteenth century psychology and needlecraft but nonetheless I do get to stimulate my mind with modules of different topics. My point is not to attempt to impress you with my academic achievements but to impress upon you this idea of trying something different or, if that's too much of a shake to your comfort zone, to try the same thing but in a slightly different way. The result is that these new or altered behaviours help to change the way our brain is wired and in turn, help to change the way that we think about things. It has long been known that our mood is affected by our environment and especially the music we listen to. Studies have been conducted which demonstrated how listening to upbeat music can increase episodes of road rage in drivers, for example, whilst listening to classical music has been shown in seemingly endless studies on the subject, to calm mood and promote relaxed behaviours - and yes, to help reduce both the frequency and severity of road rage. Interestingly some studies comparing the effects of listening to individualised music; that is music which the individual would prefer listening to, compared to classical music, have shown that individualised music reduces agitation and distress in those with dementia and cognitive impairment, for example. All of this really just proves that music is therapeutic and that what suits one person, doesn't suit all. Regardless of the style, if the music we listen to can have such a dramatic effect on our own behaviour then so, too, can our own decision to change our behaviour. Why sit there wringing our hands, grinding our teeth and puffing our cheeks out while the rapid, boundless notes of Mozart blares out of the speakers, waiting for it to take effect like some junky hit of holistic therapy, when we can actively choose to calm down, react differently and control our behaviour?

I've worked with thousands of individuals and groups of people, all over the world and from all walks of life to achieve things they didn't think were possible. My company's coaching programme helps people to step outside of their comfort zone every single day and the greatest hurdle seems to be the mere concept of this protected, imprisoned set of values, which we refer to as the comfort zone. It's got more than just a name similarity to the Twilight Zone. In fact, I think Disney could have done better than the Twilight Zone Tower of Terror, to appeal to even more people by creating the Comfort Zone Tower of Terror: a ride of mirrors which show you what you could have had and what you could be doing, followed by that rapid, stomach-churning drop to emulate that rush of gut-wrenching anxiety when you're faced with doing something "outside of your comfort zone." Just like the notion of root canal treatment, end of year exams, driving tests and appointments to see your tremor-ridden proctologist, the somewhat mystical comfort zone gets far too much imagination space than it deserves. All of this talk about doing things "outside of the box" or "outside of our comfort zone" only helps to exacerbate the problem. I take a very bold line when it comes to zones of comfort or any other - I ban them. The words are banned, therefore, they do not exist. There is no such thing as a comfort zone. Read that last sentence over and over to yourself at least ten times. All that matters is how we respond to the challenges that present in our lives and to the people we find ourselves with, environments we end up in and the day to day changes to the here and now. If you ever find yourself feeling anxious about the situation you're in, or about a potential new behaviour, such as a charity bungee jump, for example (back out now, they're as scary as being left alone with your Mother-in-law who found out through somebody else that her daughter is pregnant), then remember that the only reason that little feeling of anxiety present is because you're scared. We fear the unknown because - well, it's unknown. It's a perfectly natural emotion and what kept our species alive. Pity it kept so many of us alive frankly, but there you have it. So get over it. You've got a choice, remember: you can jump on the worry train and let that fear take you on a roller coaster so wild and fast that you'll be throwing up the contents of your stomach in no time, or you can choose not to ride. You can choose to ask yourself the question: how do I want to feel? How do I want to respond to this? How should I respond to this? What action should I take and what are the consequences of those actions? I don't even think it's about having courage or anything as dramatic as that, either. It's about making the judgement that something else is more important than the emotion you feel right now. The key to change, is to let go of fear and the more dramatic and less controlled you allow a situation to become, the greater the negative consequence on your own behaviour and in turn those that are affected, too.

What's Yours?

I'm sat today typing at my kitchen table. We've not long had our house completely renovated and this is probably only the fourth day that the house has been 99.9% finished. It's suddenly immediately relaxing to not have to consider contractors and for the house to feel clean and for the first time in two years, like home. That's a big thing for me; I'm a really homely person. Given the choice, I'd nearly always choose to stay at home rather than go out and that's probably born from the sheer amount of travel and time away from home I've spent over the past ten years working across the UK and through Europe and beyond. It's a bright October day and autumn is beginning to settle in. The leaves are falling and it's no longer warm enough to leave the doors open; instead a gentle rush of cool, fresh air trickles through the few windows I have open. Despite the temperature outside being a cool twelve degrees, I am that person who "was born in a barn." In all of the cars I've owned I think I've used air conditioning no more than five times and that's normally when Mrs Jez is in the car because the noise of the air through the windows hurts her ears. Don't ask, I don't understand either. I can't get enough of fresh air. I think that's also a result of both growing up in the Buckinghamshire countryside and the amount of time I spend in cars, airports, planes, trains and hotels and conference rooms. I remember the first time I was invited to perform on a cruise ship. It was the Queen Mary 2 and I spent nearly twenty five minutes trying to work out how to open the window in my cabin. I even called my Mum to ask for some sage advice - retrospectively that seems pointless because she's never even been on a cruise ship but such is the power of ingrained behaviours. It was my Mum who informed me that the window wouldn't open because my cabin had a port hole, not a window. So I spent the ten days at sea taking really deep breaths on the deck until eleven o'clock at night, to preserve as much fresh air in my body as possible, before heading down into my bunker, I mean cabin, for the night. I set my alarm especially early each morning to rush up to the deck and repeat the process.

As I sit here typing, I wonder about you. I know we've never met but I always think about the person who might read my book; your story, your personal circumstance. I think a lot about what might make you tick and what your extraordinary journey might be. I'd really like you to promise me one thing, okay? Whatever you do as a result of reading this book. even if it helps only a tiny bit towards your end goal, I'd really love to hear about it, okay? Get in touch with me and tell me about your journey from ordinary to extraordinary - I really enjoy hearing about other people's lives and it'll do you good to bask, for a moment, in your achievements. I believe that now is the time for you to reassess what gets you up in the morning; what drives you, inspires you and motivates you. Why now? Why not?! In reality, I know that if you don't do it now, you won't do it! You have my permission to continue holding the book while you look out of the window dreamily. I hope it's raining where you are right now, so that it adds to the effect. If you happen to be sat on a train and it's raining outside, which has resulted in the windows in your carriage slightly fogging up then even better! I am delighted for your movie moment. Consider what it is that made you get up this morning; what made the difference between staying in that cosy snuggle pit and bracing the chilled morning air outside of your duvet?

Did you have to go to work? Why? If you didn't I imagine you would get in trouble with your boss. And as a result of getting in trouble with your boss, you could lose your job perhaps. So on the face of it the reason you got up this morning was not because of your boss but through a fear that you may lose your job, if you didn't get up. However, consider this. Why do you go to work? To earn money? Why do you need to earn money? To pay your bills? Why do you need to pay your bills? Otherwise you'd be without food, electricity, a home etc.? Why do you need those things? To make you happy. So in fact you got up this morning because staying in bed wouldn't help to ensure your long-term happiness. We have a choice as to how we see and understand the things that happen to us and it's absolutely worth your while to consider this - look dreamily out of the window for as long as you need then come back to this: I'll be still here, waiting for you to read on. That's a very strange thought.

Creating extraordinary moments in our lives, doing extraordinary things with them and being extraordinary in our views, opinions, thoughts and actions, inevitably means changing our own behaviour. Once you've reconsidered what gets you up in the mornings, I believe this next piece of advice could well change everything for you. It may not, of course, however, it's an extremely powerful and enlightening exercise, which I ask most of my coaching clients to do. I've conducted this experiment with large groups of business people, sales forces, leadership teams and even school teachers. It often resonates deeply with those who do it and has a deeper impact on their behaviour than they first imagined. Try it for yourself:

Your Life A-B Split Test

Grab a piece of paper, or use one of the blank pages at the end of this book. At the top of one side, write the letter 'A'. On this piece of paper, write down all of the words and phrases that come to mind when you consider where you are in your life right now emotionally, physically, psychologically: how you feel, who you are, what you do. You can do this kind of split test for any manner of things; your personal life, work, a business dilemma or even something specific like your physical health - anything at all. I'll assume that you'll combine both work and personal life as that is what most people do when the task is to reflect on where they, as a person, are right now. You might write: anxious, concerned, worried about losing job, confused, happy, overweight - anything that describes where you are right now in your life. Don't write things that concern your dreams or aspirations - take your time to carefully consider it honestly and just write down what's real right now.

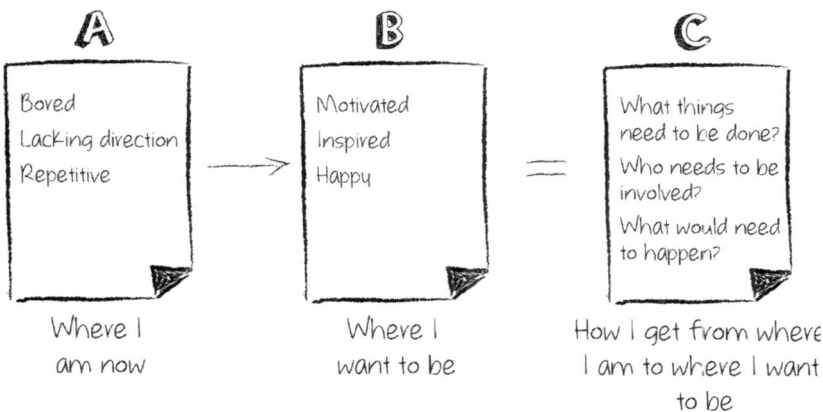

Once you've done that, find a new piece of paper and at the top write the letter 'B'. Repeat the same exercise but this time jot down anything that helps describe where you want to be: how do you want to feel?, who do you want to be?, how should you feel?, what do you want to be doing? Again, take time to seriously consider this and be honest with yourself - there are no limitations and this exercise is personal to you; no one else needs to see it. So, if you are currently a size 50 and you want to be a size 10; write it down. However, you absolutely must start with the first part of the exercise; the 'A' part. Most people are concerned with what could be in their lives: most of us have considered what we would do if we won the lottery, or given thought to what our dream house would look like or imagined ourselves doing something we aspire to do, whether that be volunteering in Uganda or driving a supercar, such are the diverse aspirations of the human condition. However, while dreaming is an important part of psychological development, it won't get you any closer to what you aspire to unless you have first carefully considered your position right now. You cannot begin to make a journey to where you wish to be if you don't know where you currently are.

On a third piece of paper, write the letter 'C' at the very top. This is the part that requires some time, active reflection and an open mind. On this piece of paper you write the things that need to happen in order to get from your 'A', where you are right now, to your 'B'; where you would like to be. What needs to change in your life? What more of some things do you need to do? What less of other things do you need to do? Who do you need to connect with or contact? Only by setting out clearly what the difference is between where you are and where you want to be, will you be able to clearly define what needs to happen in order to get you there. Once you've tried this, you'll get the hang of it and see how practical and useful it is for many different areas of your life, whenever you will benefit from clarity and an objective approach.

Deal with What's Real

Deal with what's real - drop what's not. I made that up recently, while I was driving somewhere in the car and at the time was really pleased with myself. I've just typed it out here and have to admit I did cringe. I've kept it in because it is true; I just wish I'd thought of a slightly less geeky way to say it. Today it's raining outside. It's overcast and windy and with the lights off, it's dull and dreary. However, for me it's my favourite kind of day. Light a candle, brew a pot of tea and pop a side light on and my home is magically transformed into a safe haven. As I look out of the large dining room window, I see nature doing what it does best and am thankful to be in the relative warm; my mood lifted by the flickering candle and my cup of tea. It's the simple things - but the things that help to transform my day from grey to great are the parts that I put in place. I've changed how I feel today by taking charge of my environment and that's something not enough people do. I call them the back-seat moaners because while other people like me are in the driving seat, taking control of their day and the consequences of their actions, other people just sit in the back moaning that it's cold, or wet or that they're bored. Put a jumper on or turn the heating up. Get an umbrella or a waterproof coat but do something! All of that oxygen they've wasted. What happens if they get hit by a bus (come on, we're all thinking it)? They'll have less oxygen to save them! Which isn't necessarily all that much of a problem (oh come on, I know you were thinking that, too!). It's those back-seat moaners that we come across in daily life who have helped shape my, all-be-it somewhat embarrassing mantra of "deal with what's real - drop what's not." Those things which haven't happened yet, or which are inconsequential in the grand scheme of things, are often not worth spending time on; they hold you back and prevent you from spending time and energy on the things that really matter. For example, while you're moaning about being cold, you could be actively doing something about it to change the situation and moving forwards, progressing with your goals or life.

It's not just about jumpers and umbrellas though, of course. If we all take a moment to consciously monitor our responses to our environment and our reactions to those around us, in an attempt to catch ourselves spending time or energy on the things that we can actively do something about. We can literally train our brain to be more proactive, whilst simultaneously getting more done, realising our own happiness quicker and being more efficacious in our approach to our work life, home life and personal development. The things that affect us here and now are the things that we need to deal with; the things that might be, or that we don't have sufficient information to base a sound judgement on, or those things that we know little to nothing about, are a waste of time to worry over and spend time on. Making a decision or acting upon third hand knowledge or information from people who won't have all of the knowledge you need, is one of those "drop what's not" moments. We could spend all of our lives forming opinions, making decisions and acting upon advice based on things that aren't concrete, justified, substantiated - real. I've sat in boardrooms around large tables surrounded by senior executives while time is wasted as they engage in debate about things they don't actually need to concern themselves with just yet, because they are making assumptions and hypothesising for areas where they lack knowledge. One question from me normally brings the entire room to a standstill: "do you need to make a decision on this right now, or can it wait until you have all of the facts?" And so it should be in our own businesses, at home and in our personal lives, too because as a result we'd be so much more time-rich, so much more focused and so much more productive, getting closer to our personal and work goals.

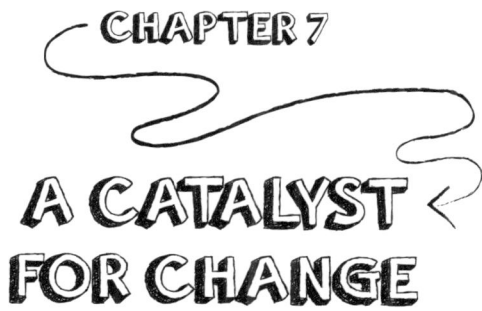

CHAPTER 7

A CATALYST FOR CHANGE

"I used to think that the worst thing in life was to end up alone. It's not. The worst thing in life is to end up with people whom make you feel alone."

Robin Williams, comedian, actor, entertainer.

This Day Shall Be Mine

I mentioned in chapter two how dementia is, for many, a cripplingly cruel disease, of loneliness, confusion and frustration. However, it doesn't have to be. The excellent work of organisations like the Contented Dementia Trust and their SPECAL method are helping to change the lives of thousands of dementia sufferers to afford them lifelong well-being.

And so it is with our lives; they don't have to be as they are right now. Far too many people tip toe through life with all the certainty of a haemophiliac in a razor-blade factory, neither confident, nor sure of who they are or where they are going. We do not have to be trapped in a suffocating state of ordinary. We have great potential; each one of us and our individual strengths are others' weaknesses. And vice versa. That's one of the things my Grandma was always fascinated by: people's stories. She would get drawn in by learning more about the rich tapestry of the lives of others and no doubt draw inspiration and much joy from hearing what other people had achieved and what they aspired to achieve. In the ten years that I've been travelling the world, speaking to organisations about changing behaviour and how to develop higher performance, I have bared witness to just how we self-limit ourselves and other people. Sitting in a conference room at a company head offices in Germany, I listen as senior board members tell me, confidentially and carefully, their unique problems of ebbing morale and disengaged staff teams. They explain in thorough detail to ensure I understand fully the challenges they face and more often than not one of them will incoherently suggest a need for "motivation," "focus," "clarity," "thinking outside of the box" and "empowerment." These words sound inspiring but like most things, are vacuous statements that make people temporarily feel better; they do not change situations. Understanding what the words mean doesn't really help much either as without knowing how to apply them and when - and what else is needed to maximise the effect - makes them all rather useless, in my opinion. I then travel to another meeting, at a different company's head offices, in a different location and meet with a similar team of managers who tell me essentially the same things about their apparently unique challenges. This has been happening for the last ten years of my life and while unique factors do exist and occasionally I meet an organisation with genuinely different challenges, largely you can count on one thing: wherever there are people, the same challenges exist. That isn't important and worth too much focus though. What is infinitely more important is finding ways to improve or solve the situations those people are in, that helps to make their lives more engaging and rewarding.

I sat in a coffee shop drinking hot water (I don't drink coffee and once you've drank loose leaf tea, you just can't go back to bags), listening to two elderly women on the table next to me. One of them was dripping in costume jewelry and made Liberace look dowdy and the other had a squeaky shoe and was ferociously opinionated; she spoke with an air of ultimate, omnipotent authority as though she and she alone had the answers to life and all of the daily news items flowed through her first. The one with the tiara and the ring on every finger accepted this self-appointed authority on face value. For these two women, everything – and I mean everything – was a problem. The coffee wasn't strong enough, was not hot enough and there was insufficient milk. The plates were a little on the small size for a slice of cake that big; the table was too close to the window; the waitresses' hair was a little untidy; there was a "distinct and problematic draught" (which I couldn't feel at all) and the frosting on the cake was nothing like they made, so they called over the waitress (the one whose uniform needed "a jolly good press," not the one with the messy hair) and gave the stunned girl a lesson in how to make frosting that was "altogether more tasteful, with a more correct consistency." It was enough to intimidate Mary Berry. I pitied these two women. What must it be like to live in a world where you think that everyone else has got it wrong? As they droned on and on and on and on and on about the many problems with the youth of today; the National Health Service; education; politicians; the police; bakeries; local authorities and the modern trend for leaving lights on, not once did they either stop to consider how negative and bitter they sounded, or to offer solutions. Instead, they grew more irritable with every sip of cold coffee and nibble of tasteless cake. They didn't have to stay did they? More's the pity that they did.

I appreciate and reflect almost daily on the very fortunate life I have and the position I am in. I have been paid to travel the world and speak to literally hundreds of thousands of people, ranging from investment bankers, vets and lorry drivers, to entrepreneurs, doctors and sales forces. And in that time, I've learnt that one thing unites these people from wildly different industries, on varying salaries and with very different responsibilities. They all want to earn money to provide for their family. They want to enjoy their job. They want to be happy. Contrary to popular belief, they largely don't want lots of money. Jessie J had it right; it really isn't about the price tag. Most sensible people recognise that having large salaries doesn't solve basic life issues, health problems or family challenges. As a social experiment, try offering someone who is inherently unhappy with their job a huge pay rise. Even a one million pound annual salary won't guarantee you job security or happiness and if you aren't able to get on with the people you work with, or are uninspired or overly pressured by your workload, no amount of money is going to balance that. While research has shown that winning the lottery can make you happier and in many more cases has positive effects rather than negative, it isn't about the money per-se. The large amounts of money from a lottery win enable you to stop working, pick and choose who you hang around with and what you do; you aren't tied to the same job where you don't get along with your boss or are continually frustrated by poor IT systems and a broken photocopier. Furthermore, large amounts of money don't protect us from personal or family tragedies, either. So, it is in fact up to us to make the best out of the situations we are presented with; to focus on exactly what it is we want to do more of - or less of - and try harder to ensure we find that for ourselves, or indeed create it for others. Thomas Heath Flood wrote: "This day shall be mine. From the first gray streak of its early dawn till the last golden ray of its setting sun melts away on the horizon of the West, it shall belong to me... I will live so that should tomorrow dawn, I may look upon to-day with a feeling that I have added my humble mite to the cause of Justice and Humanity." You could do worse for inspiration to focus your outlook and sense of purpose.

What people really want is purpose. It's the one consistent across our race. The board members, senior executives and managers I work with all have a duty to help ensure happiness and a sense of wellbeing in those who work for them, in order to get the best out of their staff and to develop higher performance in them. They have a responsibility to provide them with a sense of purpose. The commercially savvy ones recognise the wider commercial implications of doing so, too. However, if we're all honest about it, we are all guilty of looking for the easy option in most things in life. We're a species of magic wand seekers; we all want the pill or the diet or even the person that will do the hard work for us: we don't actively work at our marriages or seek knowledge on how to be better parents; we use fear, intimidation and violence in favour of patience and peace. So it appears much easier to just give people a pay rise and hope that will make them happy instead of taking the time to find out what they find motivating and reinforcing and to ask what happens in their job that makes them want to leave. The long-term benefits of behaviour change take consideration and a little more effort and thought to work out. It is those individuals and organisations who recognise the additional effort they put in to regular appraisals, soliciting feedback, developing an inclusive team and seeking out suggestions for ways to improve helps to create a higher performing, extraordinary team. So, is the key to being extraordinary simply a case of thinking differently and putting in additional effort? Clearly it is more than that because applying extra effort to the wrong areas and at the wrong time, for example, would not necessarily yield extraordinary results. But there does appear to be one consistent in all of the extraordinary acts, people and results I've researched: thinking differently. Not allowing yourself to be restricted by what has gone before you and to dare to try something different, accepting that you might have been wrong or that it may not work but that the result is not all that tragic in the grand scheme of things compared to the payoff if it works. I don't believe that by doing so makes you a maverick, nor does it encourage you to actively go against the grain just for the sake of doing so. It does, however, give you the freedom to decide for yourself that you won't be actively confined to the way others think; to be restricted to following the same ideals, methods and ways of working as others and to look bleakly around you and ask, in a hushed and hopeful voice: "Is this it? Is this all there is?"

Oscar Wilde wrote: "to live is the dearest thing in the world. Most people exist, that is all." My experience echoes Wilde's opinion: most people exist (and I'm sure you've met a few, as I have, that you think really shouldn't) and while that is fine if it is their choice, most people exist and do not even know they are doing so. They accept life as it is; a simple series of events: of waking, some activity in the middle, which includes some eating and bodily functions, then sleeping. Then they wake up again and rinse and repeat. We can always make more money – but we'll never get any more time. Grab a piece of paper and a pen, or if you can only find a pen or pencil, you'll find some blank pages at the back of the book for you to make notes. The average lifespan of an adult male in England, at the time of writing, is 78.9 years and 82.9 years for an adult female, according to Public Health England. There are twelve months in a year, which means women will live for an average of 994.8 months and men for 946.8 months. How old are you right now? Let's assume you're 30. Multiply your age by 12, to get the number of months that you've been alive so far. If you're 30, it's 360 (I've done it for you). Now subtract the number of months you've been alive (in this example 360), from your average monthly life span (I'm a male, so my calculation would be 946.8 – 360). The answer (in this example 586.8) is how many months you have, on average, left to live. It's a sobering thought, isn't it?

It's your choice what you do with your time but all of those that we've known, loved and lost, no longer have that time available to them. But we do. It's our responsibility, surely, to make the most of what we have left? Gwendoline Pearl Cunliffe was the perfect catalyst for extraordinary. Now it's your turn - be extraordinary.

AFTERWORD

In 2007 my life took a monumental change of direction. I found myself sat staring at the plain walls of a small room in the Spinal Injury Unit of Sheffield Northern General following an accident during one of my horse riding competitions. I now had a life-changing burden hanging over me – I was no longer able to walk, let alone compete in any riding events, for the rest of my life.

It's not uncommon to hear that the biggest difficulty someone faces with becoming paraplegic is not just the day-to-day living with being paralysed chest down, but the internal struggle you have with yourself to come back with a fighting determination. It's all too easy to let it defeat you.

It is this exact point that is addressed so beautifully by Jez; how to become great. He makes you realise that by using a few simple techniques you can truly empower yourself by achieving so much more than you ever thought possible. It doesn't matter which extreme you approach it from; whether, like me, you are returning after something like a life-changing accident, or you are making your comeback after a slight dip in your career, through reading Be a Purple Banana, you can be extraordinary.

I don't doubt for one second that any reader of Be a Purple Banana has learnt that 'being extraordinary' is not just the principle focus of the book, but a fundamental life lesson that can benefit anyone who puts it into action. From here, see how much you can now grow and become the absolute best you can be, even when faced with seemingly crushing setbacks. Although at the time my accident was totally devastating, I have now achieved things I wouldn't have done if it wasn't for that day that changed my life. When I was at school my worst nightmare was speaking in front of the class, now I am a speaker and love it. I would never have believed this. Never say never. Becoming paralsyed has made me do things I would have thought were not possible.

The one thing I've learned over the years is that to achieve any goal you set yourself and to really achieve results, you must not only believe in your ability to achieve it, but to be prepared. Often, being prepared mentally can be just as, if not more, important than the necessary physical preparation. I was 32 years old (and paraplegic for five of those years) when I decided to take on the immense task of completing the Virgin London Marathon using the ReWalk bionic suit. Yes, it was an extremely harrowing experience physically trying to walk 26 miles when in reality I couldn't walk at all. But it was the small hurdles that I struggled with the most like trying to lift my legs over pavements that are often very bumpy and uneven. I took each step of my 17- day journey as it came in the same way I have done for the past eight years since my accident.

My journey has been tough but extremely rewarding and I know everyone reading this will have embarked on their own extraordinary journey through life – a journey which is subjective and entirely unique to you. Whatever yours is, use the *Be a Purple Banana* principles to focus, achieve and drive that ambition further each day. Take heed of Jez's invaluable advice and use the book to remind yourself that you really are capable of so much more than you believe you are right now. Try it - be extraordinary.

Claire Lomas
Campaigner, Fundraiser and Speaker.

SOMETHING SPECIAL THIS WAY COMES

I'm very grateful that you have read my book. As a massive thank you for buying *Be a Purple Banana*, I'd like to offer you something very special, which, if you enjoyed this book, I think you're going to really enjoy; it's a look inside the workings of my mind!

I've been creating and delivering training programmes and materials to help individuals and organisations to develop higher performance for almost 12 years and in that time have produced a huge amount of highly effective resources including printed materials, video series, Webinars, podcasts and articles. For the first time ever, I am launching a very special training programme called the High Performance Programme, especially designed to get extraordinary results from ordinary people.

Keep an eye on www.HighPerformanceProgramme.com for an exciting launch mid-2015!

MY PERSONAL GUARANTEE

For ten years I've read and researched self-help books and spent time applying the results of scientific research and my own research, to the efficacy of the techniques and claims laid out within those books. *Be a Purple Banana* is a resource to change the way you think; to shift your mindset from thinking about things in a less ordinary way and to see the sensational benefits - for you and others - when you begin to think extraordinarily.

If by the end of the book, having read all of it, you genuinely don't feel or think any differently, then I've not achieved what I set out to. I'm very grateful for you having spent your hard-earned money on my book and would hate for there to be that disappointed feeling at the end, where you're left feeling a little empty. I've been there with books I've bought. So, if that's you, please do return your copy, along with your receipt, and we will refund the amount you paid in full. This will not affect the charitable donation we made on your behalf when you purchased the book. You'll never get the time back you spent reading it, but I know that even at a subconscious level, many of the points within the book will be working away and you'll notice a tangible difference in the not too distant future.

However, I wrote this book with a view that you'd feel different by the end of it and if that hasn't happened, parcel your copy up, along with your receipt and send to:

Be a Purple Banana Book
Dr. Zeus Ltd
c/o 7 Merlin Centre
Aylesbury
Buckinghamshire
HP19 8DP

Be sure to include your name and address,
otherwise we won't be able to fulfil your refund.

ACKNOWLEDGEMENTS

It would be fantastically remiss of me not to start by publicly giving very special thanks to Steve Penson, Adam Briggs, Franziska Dodl and Eve Nichols, without whom, this book quite literally would not have been finished. They were the people involved in searching for my memory stick with the only saved copy of my book on, when, like a complete idiot, I lost it. Thank you all for your efforts and for sympathising so genuinely.

As any author will tell you, usually only one name appears on the cover of their book, yet there are many people involved in getting a book to be in your hands. Some have direct roles and others help more than they could ever imagine, indirectly. I'd like to publicly acknowledge the fantastic work of my assistant, Steph Middleton-Foster, who so efficiently manages my diary, among many other things so efficiently and professionally, which provided me with the protected time I needed to write. In the same light, my manager Kenny Donaldson is something of a rare find indeed and I am indebted to his professionalism, support and guidance. Having a good manager is not the icing on the cake but the solid foundations and he and Jean have unfalteringly embraced an, at times, challenging client! I am very grateful to those who gave up their time to discuss with me ideas or be interviewed by me for this book: Richard McDougall, Robert Williams and David Goodfellow. Special thanks to Louise Thompson Davies, Alinda and Kent Coffman at Kellogg's for their time researching the heritage of the Variety Pack. And to Tom Bryson, forever now known as Gandhi, for his permission to use the photograph of him outside a Manchester hotel in the middle of a fire evacuation. Sincerest thanks of course to those who contributed to this book: David Berglas for finding the time in a very busy schedule to write an inspiring preface. I must publicly acknowledge David as the mastermind behind, among other relevant suggestions, the revised title "Getting Extraordinary Results From Ordinary People (Or *Be a Purple Banana*)," which appears on the paperback edition. And no thanks to David would be complete without thanking him and his wife Ruth for their magical hospitality. I am indebted to Sir Ranulph Fiennes for finding the time in an especially hectic schedule while completing his own book and preparing for his next expedition, to write the foreword - I could think of no one more fitting to head up a book about getting extraordinary results than him and the maxim of asking a busy person really could not apply more to Sir Ranulph! Caroline Robertson introduced me to Claire Lomas and her quite extraordinary journey and I'm delighted she did. Thank you Caz. Claire's journey puts a perfect metaphorical full stop at the end of the book I hope it inspires you to never give up.

Of course my editor Wendy Mansfield who has helped pull my thoughts together into something that is more readable and congruent than when it started. There is no way that one person could produce the output that we achieve and I am so grateful and proud of the team that works alongside me, in addition to those already mentioned: Claire Speight for her excellent cover artwork and for typesetting, as well as all of the other fantastic graphical work she does, Matt Hulbert for his keen editing and design eye and for working like a trojan, always. Emily du Feu and Rebecca Morris for managing the sometimes frenetic administration workload and so competently handling the seemingly never ending task list and orders.

Thanks must also go to a few people who have invited me to share and work with them on some fantastic events for some really awesome clients, many of whom we still work with: Julie Albury of Smart Talk, Catherine Turner of Catherine Turner Productions, Jillie Bushell of Jillie Bushell Associates, Gemma Texeira of KTS Events and Katharina Fenzl and Silke Jerger from Proske.

Extra special thanks must go here to Marc Paul, without whom I would never have met the wonderful man and legend that is David Berglas, nor the exceptionally talented Tony Nicholson and started my journey into television. I'm not going to list the many friends and colleagues I've met in television, for fear of this reading like a whose who of who's on screen (or not, depending on when you're reading this). However, public thanks must go to John Kaye Cooper and Tony Humphries for their belief and trust in me.

To my clients; past, present and future, I thank you for working with The Behaviour Expert and for embracing behaviour change. In some cases those changes have been significant and, such is the nature of behaviour, not always smooth. To see and share with you the results of higher performance is a joy and the core purpose of why we do what we do, so thank you for having that intrigue, that belief and making the leap of faith to do something about it. I'd like to extend special thanks to Sucheet Amin at Aequitas Legal, Dominic Timney and Lindsey Harbour at Boehringer Ingelheim, Amanda O'Reilly at Worthing Theatres, Matthew Barham at Volkswagen UK, the team at HBOS (we had fun, didn't we?!), Chris Auty and Philip Stores of Unitron and Penny Cole, Jayne Young, Tracey Hahn, Craig Travers and Paul Feeney of Old Mutual Wealth. And to the individuals who I coach, for challenging and stretching me and allowing me to be a part of your personal and professional development. As I type this, you are: Hilary, Mitch, Karen, Dom, Sian, Joe, Naomi, Emma, Chris, David, Andy, Lucy, Lisa and Dan.

Every book has at least one and sometimes three people who you know you have to list because otherwise you will be forever plagued by their incessant moaning at not having had a mention. In my case those three are Sian Nisbett, Melanie Poynter and Laura Moxham They just so happen to also be three of the finest women I know in business and I get great pleasure for having been a part of their journeys and for them being a part of mine. On the subject of journeys, all-be-it of a more physical nature, I'd like to thank my driver, Dan, for making so many miles and hours so much more bareable.

I absolutely must give heartfelt thanks to Mrs Jez. She is the perfect companion. Always so patient with my workload, which can often be quite heavy and occasionally hectic. Writing this book has happened whilst a number of personal and professional challenges presented themselves, some of which you'll recognise that I've shared with you and during that time Mrs Jez has, as ever, been wonderfully supportive. She is the one constant in a life of true variety and I am grateful to have her by my side. And here to my parents, too, without whom I wouldn't be here but for their patience and support: if you look up the word "understanding" in the dictionary, I expect you'll see a photo of them both. My best friend Alex Healy has been at my side for years and has so patiently journeyed with me through the many highs and lows, never failing to offer the right words and level of support at the right time. Sharing that same place is his oestrogen equivalent, Kate Collier. Without those two people in my life, it would have significantly less laughter, silliness and probably smaller credit card bills, too. The interesting thing about friendship is that there are often no words to accurately describe appreciation or even the emotional response to just hearing their names. I hope they know how much I love them dearly. Thanks must always go to Clifford Bradley who never seems to quite grasp how wonderful he is; a rare example of someone who can share a space in your heart as a friend and business confidant, I am every day grateful for his knowledge, experience and professionalism, which translates into the guidance, advice and caution he so selflessly offers. Ruth Cox; where do I begin?! Laughter, tears and trauma - that would be the title of our book if ever we wrote one. Thank you for being such a wonderful inspiration and for giving me the opportunity to know and care for the best Goddaughter in the world. No page of acknowledgements would be complete without mentioning my second mother, Judith Kaye. A force not to be reckoned with that I'm so grateful to have reckoned with.

The team at the Contented Dementia Trust, my adopted charitable partner cannot go unmentioned. Their tireless, dedicated, constant work to bring a greater sense of well-being to those living with dementia is, frankly, awe-inspiring. I've learnt so much in the relatively short time I've been working with them and never cease to be excited about the SPECAL method and their deep belief in changing the way that those with dementia live.

And finally to you, for your intrigue and for reading this far. Thank you. Now stop reading about people you don't know and start your journey to extraordinary.

RESOURCES

Websites

The Behaviour Expert
www.thebehaviourexpert.com

Sir Ranulph Fiennes
www.ranulphfiennes.co.uk

Claire Lomas
www.claireschallenge.co.uk

The Contented Dementia Trust
www.contenteddementiatrust.org

Breathe Magic Project
www.breatheahr.org

The Kindness Offensive
www.thekindnessoffensive.com

My TEDx Talk on the subject of
'Generosity, Greed and The Greater Good':
http://bit.ly/tedxmk

TED
www.ted.com

Books

Have A Crap Day by Jez Rose
ISBN: 1909093289
Available from: www.haveacrapday.com and Amazon

Contented Dementia by Dr. Oliver James
ISBN: 0091901812

We Are Our Brains by Dick Swaab
ISBN: 978-0-241-00372-5

The Brain That Changes Itself by Norman Doidge
ISBN: 978-0-141-03887-2

The following pages are intentionally
blank for your notes